HOW

Finding Yourself in the Language of Repentance

How to Be a Sinner

Finding Yourself in the Language of Repentance

P ETER B OUTENEFF

ST VLADIMIR'S SEMINARY PRESS
Yonkers · New York
2018

Library of Congress Cataloging-in-Publication Data

Names: Bouteneff, Peter, author.
Title: How to be a sinner : finding yourself in the language of repentance / Peter Bouteneff.
Description: Yonkers, NY : St . Vladimir's Seminary Press, 2018.
Identifiers: LCCN 2018000662 (print) | LCCN 2018002290 (ebook) | ISBN 9780881416244 | ISBN 9780881416237 (alk. paper)
Subjects: LCSH: Sin. | Repentance. | Theological anthropology. | Christian life. | Orthodox Eastern Church—Doctrines.
Classification: LCC BL475.7 (ebook) | LCC BL475.7 .B688 2018 (print) | DDC 234/.5—dc23
LC record available at https://lccn.loc.gov/ 2018000662

Copyright © 2018
St Vladimir's Seminary Press
575 Scarsdale Road · Yonkers · NY · 10707
1-800-204-2665
www.svspress.com

ISBN 978-0-88141-623-7 (print)
ISBN 978-0-88141-624-4 (electronic)

For Brother John

Contents

Preface

Common to most religious life is the understanding that we human beings are flawed, and that we are liable to think and do wrong. Classical Christian tradition pulls no punches when it comes to expressing what that means for me and for my plight as a human being. In our regular set prayers, we call ourselves "sinners," "wretched," "pitiful," and "worthy of condemnation." This language can sound odd or extreme to many sensibilities, yet there it is, front and center. If we accept that we are sinners, how do we understand that in a proper way? How does it help us heal and find redemption?

I have been thinking on these themes for several years. I began putting them to paper for a Lenten retreat I gave in 2015 at St Vladimir's Seminary, where I have taught for nearly twenty years. I am grateful to my colleagues, students, and former teachers there, for their support and for all they continue to teach me. Much of this book was written during several visits to New Skete, where I gained immeasurably from the monks' and nuns' hospitality and my conversations with them. I am grateful to my wife, Patricia, who to an ever-increasing degree has been my inspiring conversation partner, challenging sounding board, and generally humbling influence. She is also the best editor I've ever had. If this book is of any use to you, it's thanks to the people and communities I've mentioned, together with many others whom I love and esteem. Its faults are my own. Oh, and about those faults . . .

Introduction

Everybody sins. We all fall short of the glory of genuine human life—sometimes in small ways, sometimes in larger ways, sometimes by thinking, saying, and doing, truly terrible things. The Bible and every church service remind us of this constantly. I may ask myself, "Am I really that horrible?" I may think, "This is so negative and judgmental." Or perhaps, "Wait, am I beginning to *like* this language in a strange way?" Or else, "I've had too many people in my life tell me I'm worthless. I don't need a book and a church to add to that hateful chorus."

But if we are going to be part of the Church, we must face up to the sin within us. In the New Testament, we hear St Paul saying, "None is righteous, no, not one" (Rom 3:10). Later, we read, "If we say we are sinless we deceive ourselves" (1 Jn 1:8). We are meant to acknowledge that everyone transgresses. And that means that I sin. That I am a sinner. More starkly, as St

Paul says in another epistle, "I am the foremost of sinners" (1 Tim 1:15).

The idea goes back to the Old Testament. In prayer, we echo the psalmist,

> For I know my transgressions,
>> and my sin is ever before me.
> Against you, you alone, have I sinned,
>> and done what is evil in your sight,
> so that you are justified in your sentence
>> and blameless when you pass judgment.
> Indeed, I was born guilty,
>> a sinner when my mother conceived me.
>
> (Ps 51:3–5)

Even though the language of sin can make us uncomfortable, it also acknowledges the world as we know it.[1] It's not a stretch for most of us to see that the world is broken and that the root of the problem lies in our human inclination toward the wrong. Reinhold Niebuhr famously remarked, "Original sin is the only empirically verifiable doctrine of the Christian faith." People may not accept Christianity or the existence of a personal God. But they generally have little problem believing that our existential situation is dire.

Where do we situate ourselves in that picture? In the 1930s, someone asked the English writer and lay theologian G. K. Chesterton what was wrong with the world. He answered, "I am." The idea of each of us taking responsibility, of locating societal sin with *me,* my own self, hasn't exactly presented itself as attractive in public discourse, however. Yet public opinion on these matters is beginning to shift. An increasing number of social commentators and psychologists, secular and religious, are drawing attention to the need for a healthy understanding of sin.

Self-identifying as "a sinner" is tricky to get right. I can have healthy reasons for avoiding that identity, as it has been known to perpetuate harmful behavior or abusive relationships. Focusing on myself as a sinner risks becoming maudlin or masochistic. Yet the "sinner identity" is useful—if only to provoke us to ask ourselves some challenging questions. Am I reluctant to take a deep, critical look at my thoughts and actions? Am I afraid of humility, because it might set me back in my career ambitions? Am I just a pawn in a dominant culture of self-gratification? These questions are neither simple nor straightforward. But grappling with them can play a pivotal role in my flourishing, my inner peace, my relationship with God and the world.

The thesis of this short book is that there are realistic, useful, and healthy ways to understand ourselves within the dynamic of sin—just as there are also destructive and unhelpful ways. The goal is to help us find and walk a well-directed path through critical self-reflection, in freedom, joy, divine grace, and mercy.

As a start, let me introduce you to some people, who might sound familiar. The first two have trouble self-identifying as sinners. The third finds it too easy.

John considers himself a basically decent person. He has never seriously injured anyone. He is faithful to his wife. He goes to work, does his job, and looks after his family. He is more-or-less honest in his financial dealings. He doesn't see the point of "confessing his sins." Sure, he tells the odd lie and sometimes stares at erotic images on the internet. But he believes in God, and regards himself as a normal, reasonable person. He sometimes quotes Homer Simpson, saying "I'm not a bad guy! I work hard, and I love my kids. So why should I spend half my Sunday hearing about how I'm going to hell?"

Joanne despises herself and her life. Her parents hadn't wanted children and regularly reminded her that, if anything, they would have preferred a son. They rarely called her by her name. Her father sometimes beat her, though in other moods he was uncomfortably affectionate. Nothing that Joanne did seemed to be good enough. Her efforts always fell short of what her parents wanted. In fact, she couldn't figure out what their expectations were, given that they fluctuated between the unattainably high and the pathetically low. She sometimes cuts herself. The idea of calling herself a sinner makes her feel sick. Although she knows the term well, it represents everything she's trying to move beyond. Her therapist has advised her to have as little to do with her family and her church as possible.

Paisios joined the Church a year and a half ago. His name used to be Jim, but he's asked his friends and family to refer to him by his new Christian name. He signs his emails, even if they contain nothing more than the day's shopping list, "+ The Wretch, Paisios." He is participating in an unacknowledged contest with others as to who is the worst sinner. He dresses in black, reads ascetical literature, and has grown a flourishing beard. He goes to confession, though not to his parish priest but to a monk 250 miles away.

All of these examples represent instances of the sinner identity that need some adjustment, so as not to lead either to self-destruction or hubris. In addition, the Church's reminders of our sinfulness are at loggerheads with our current society, which encourages self-empowerment, accepting ourselves, and abolishing negative thoughts or language about ourselves. This call to self-affirmation begins early. Virtually every film aimed at children seems to hammer at the theme, "Be true to yourself; love yourself exactly as you are." Every child in a sports or academic competition receives a trophy for showing up. For people who grow up in such a culture, the Church's fixation on personal wretchedness may promise to stir up a cocktail of self-hatred, masochism, abandoning success and fulfillment, or "humbly bragging" that you are the greatest of offenders. As if it were a contest.

But society's focus on self-affirmation can carry an important truth. Self-acceptance can healthily lead us to a realistic appraisal of who we are, and reveal what is and is not changeable within us. Learning self-affirmation can be especially important if we if we have been told in our early years—by parents, teachers, school-mates—that we are pathetic or unwanted. Otherwise, we are likely to make destructive life choices and project our self-loathing onto others.

So how do we make sense of the Church's language of sin and repentance, its prayers for divine mercy on us as wretched sinners? How do some people manage to find liberation, joy, and salvation in it—and how can we tap into that? One thing is sure: God did not create us for self-hating misery. God did not make us in his image so that we could spend our lives deploring ourselves, or feeling guilty for not feeling guilty enough. He did not put us on this earth to wallow. In the second century, St Irenaeus wrote, "The glory of God is a living human being."[2] By "living" he meant a person rightly alive to the vision of God and all that is good.

Seeing ourselves as sinners means that we are also going to have to grapple with humility. That is a concept that is alternately derided and praised in our society. Some see the word as having negative connotations. They may fear that being "poor in spirit" might stop them from achieving greatness. In that light, the novelist Ayn Rand, for example, took an extreme view of humility as the root of all evil. But when we meet someone who is truly self-effacing, modest, and aware of their faults and their complete dependency on God, we actually may find that person deeply compelling, wondering what it is that gives them that freedom, confidence, and inner calm. We can sense that to be genuinely humble can be liberating. Ironically, it can be a path to greatness, to spectacular achievements. And such people are often the most peaceful, joyous, and even strongest human beings we will ever know. That's quite a distance from the clichéd image of the "humble one" as the pathetic church-mouse with bad posture and worse breath.

So my goals in this book revolve around reorienting our understanding of how to "successfully" be a sinner:

- To see a genuine "sinner identity" as realistic and healing, rather than neurotic

- To understand that identity as holistic, rather than divisive

- To cultivate a self-love that is healthy, rather than narcissistic

- To find self-acceptance that is realistic and constructive, rather than libertine

Some other goals are:

- To help you direct your heart towards healthy and genuine compunction

- To help motivate positive change and correction of your life through love

- To help make you aware of our total dependency on God

- To help show you the breadth and depth of God's love and mercy

One benefit of this reorientation (apart from the palpable experience of salvation, freedom, and lightness!) is that we will gain an understanding of ourselves before God that will make it impossible for us to judge or condemn others. That means that we might reduce by at least one person—ourself—the number of judgmental and resentful Christians, which is surely a worthy goal!

Who Is This Book For?

As I wrote this, I had in mind people of Christian faith who have had a niggling question about the Church's sinner language. It is also written for you if you are looking for ways to intensify your experience of your faith—to make it more real. As we repeat written prayers and psalms, sometimes we skim over the bits that sound foreign or else we read them in a pro-forma way. What would happen if we took that language seriously? The book is not going to demand theological expertise, only a desire to go deeper.

This book is rooted in the life of the Orthodox Church. It draws on that tradition and its sensibilities. As a result, it challenges some cherished teachings from Reformed Christianity. Those include ideas about human total depravity or predestination. The idea that a person can be saved only from the moment of belief and confession in Jesus as Lord is likewise foreign to Orthodox thinking. In our theology, humans rely completely on God for our very existence as well as for our flourishing and salvation.

We do not view humans as totally depraved. The image of God propels us to cooperate willingly in the process of our salvation and lies at our core identity, however broken that may be. A central premise of this book is that we human beings are innately good. But from the very beginning we distort this goodness and must recover it. We are sinners who, even as we are constantly being forgiven, must always be in the process of conversion and the correction of our lives. But God's grace and mercy reaches us precisely *through* our brokenness. In this, we begin to see what lies at the heart of our joy, humility, and inner liberty.

All Christian churches feature some form of public and/or private confession of sin. This book sometimes will reference the different forms of practice of private confession in the Orthodox, Roman Catholic, and other traditions. My hope is that wherever you stand within the spectrum of spiritual life, experience, and teaching, you will find the following chapters relatable and useful.

Notes

[1] For a reflection on what we mean by the word "sin," see the appendix "What is Sin?" at page 175.

[2] Irenaeus, *Against Heresies* 4.20.7.

1
Discovering Myself as "Sinner"

If we say we have no sin, we deceive ourselves, and the truth is not in us.

1 John 1.8

None is righteous, no, not one.

Romans 3.10

When I refused to confess my sin, my body wasted away.

Psalm 32.3

M ost all of us are well aware that we have faults. What we do with that knowledge is another matter. It is possible to make too little or too much of our shortcomings. We may brush them off, saying "I'm only human." Conversely we might be shocked by our faults, as a matter of pride. "How can someone as wonderful as I am get it so wrong?" Some of us will experience real self-loathing and become disasters to ourselves as well as to everyone around us. Any of us are liable to move along the spectrum between these two extreme reactions at different points in our lives. But apart from the emotional aspect of dealing with our faults, we need to try to take an objective look at ourselves. Just as we need to diagnose an illness so that it can be treated, we have to find a way to perceive our wrong-headedness, misdeeds, and skewed priorities. We need to acknowledge and take responsibility for them. This is crucial for our mental, physical, and spiritual health.

In this book we are going to devote considerable attention to the potential pitfalls of sinner language, which can include toxic levels of guilt and shame. They can also cause us to forget the innate glory of humanness. But probably the more common phenomenon is the person who doesn't believe that sinner language relates to him, the "basically decent person" who cannot conceive that he or she is in desperate need of divine healing, of reconciliation with God, others, and the created world.

Knowledge of yourself—especially your sins—is vital to your health. A full self-understanding is extremely rare, if not unattainable. According to St Isaac the

Syrian, seeing ourselves as we really are is a greater miracle than raising the dead.[1] So in this chapter we will talk about how to discover ourselves as sinners. This discovery, not surprisingly, is always a process. Ideally, we are always growing into a deeper understanding of ourselves in relation to God and each other. Self-discovery, including that of our sinner identity, is a journey. Most of us don't wake up one day crying out, as the psalmist does, "For I know my transgressions, and my sin is ever before me" (Ps 51.3). Most of us are able to live into its words only gradually. This voyage, like any other, will take us through peaks and valleys.

One Journey

Self-discovery by definition is a personal matter. It is private and it looks different for everyone. That said, I thought it might be helpful to walk you through my own, as an example.

I can't point to the day and hour that I began to see myself as a sinner. But I could narrow it down to about a five-year period in my youth, with a "before" picture and an "after" picture. Part of the "before" was that once I turned seven, there was never a time when I didn't go to confession at least a few times a year. I would typically confess that I lied, I fought with my sister, I got angry, or whatever. I knew that these actions were "sins." I never considered myself a saint or a particularly good person. I had plenty of insecurities. I knew I surely wasn't getting things right. I knew in my core I believed in God, and loved him and the Church, and that I fell short of being worthy of either. Despite that, it didn't occur to me to apply to call myself "a sinner." I had no clear concept for what that word meant, and no idea how to evaluate it as a word that might describe myself. I pushed it to one side: "sinner" sounded too negative, and perhaps a little too pious. Plus I figured that I was basically a decent guy.

Then occurred a confession when I was in my early 20s. Very little had come to me to say that day. I knew that it somehow wasn't right to say so little—to feel so little—about my wrongful thoughts, words, acts. I knew I had to be erring more than I was conscious of. (Not to mention that other people's confessions always seem to take so much more time than mine!) So I said all of that to the priest. He said, very matter-of-factly and without special portent, "It's all right, Peter. Sometimes God hides our sinfulness from us. He puts a cloak over our sins. Especially when he knows we couldn't bear to see them."

As you can imagine, that got me thinking—for a few years.

My long transition period included two years living in Japan and traveling throughout Asia. On my trek homeward, I spent several weeks in the tumultuous tranquility of different monasteries in Greece and England that daily recited the Jesus Prayer for hours at a time. "Lord, Jesus Christ, Son of God, have mercy on me, a sinner." The wording of that prayer varies from community to community. Interestingly—and coincidentally—the monasteries where I stayed the longest used a wording of the Jesus Prayer that omitted the word "sinner." I know that my sojourns in those communities profoundly helped shape my understanding of myself as a sinner, though not by using that word in that prayer. Maybe just asking for God's *mercy*, over and over again, presupposes that you need it pretty desperately.

Within months of those monastic stays, I started studying at seminary. By that time the sinner language had somehow come together in a way that made sense to me. After all those years, the penny finally dropped. But the journey didn't end there. It continues in what I hope is a constantly deepening understanding of my fallen state and my utter dependence on God, his mercy, forgiveness, and love.

* * *

Your story will be different from mine. Everyone's is, and relatively few will involve sojourns at monasteries and seminaries. But in reviewing my experience and that of others, I can point to several factors that can help soften our hearts and sharpen our self-perception. These might help bring you to the discovery that you are a sinner—a forgiven sinner. Let's look at what the experience of beauty, purity, truth, and light can do.

Exposure

Have you ever found yourself in the presence of someone who fills you with light and good? In that presence, have you perhaps simultaneously felt somehow exposed and ashamed? You don't even have to exchange words with someone like that, to know that you are in the presence of holiness. People—or places—that are pure, transparent, holy can simultaneously inspire and expose us. They give us an inkling of what it might feel like to experience the presence of God. Can we endure that degree of love and beauty?

St Paul tells us to think about whatever is true, honorable, just, pure, lovely, worthy of praise (Phil 4.8). Why? Because they are intimations of God. They describe Jesus Christ. They are a window to his presence. They soften our hearts. Their brilliance fills us and can act as a spotlight on our lowliness and failings. St Paul challenges us: "Walk as children of light, for the fruit of light is found in all that is good and right and true." He continues, "When anything is exposed by the light it becomes visible, for anything that becomes visible is light" (Eph 5.8–13).

Our feelings when we encounter with beauty, truth, purity may describe arcs of greater and lesser proportions, tracing heights and depths of feeling, often simultaneously. "Lord, it is good to be here!" exclaims Peter upon seeing Jesus clothed in uncreated Light, just before he is overcome by the sight. After he and the others fall on their faces in awe, Jesus tells them to rise and stop being afraid (Mt 17.2–7).

A crucial moment in the story of Mary of Egypt (4th–5th c.) came when she put herself in the presence of the cross of Christ and an icon of the Virgin Mary. As a far-gone sex addict standing in front of holiness, salvation, and purity, she was brought to the stark recognition of how polluted her life was, such that she couldn't even enter the church. In her repentance, she began to experience a feeling—not of divine judgment, but of mercy. And so she began her decades-long odyssey to completely change her life.

The great 20th-century poet W. H. Auden reflected on his friendship with the Christian writer Charles Williams in this way:

> I had met many good people before who made me ashamed of my own shortcomings, but in the presence of this man . . . I did not feel ashamed. I felt transformed into a person who was incapable of doing or thinking anything base or unloving.[2]

He is describing what ideally happens when we place ourselves in front of goodness: not destructive shame, but the sense of possibility. The built-in potential for good is ultimately a sense of the true inner self. It contains the sense of how sin is utterly contrary to that inner self.

Our exposure to anything that is really true, genuine, beautiful—or to someone who loves us completely, to the core of our being—can be a terrifying experience. We may want to turn tail and run, fast, because we know that to withstand that exposure entails the changing our life. The pain of this experience is only tolerable when we know that we are being "judged" by someone who is pure love and mercy. And God is loving and merciful to an extent that is beyond our comprehension.

Sometimes we needn't travel far to experience that kind of exposure. In fact, we can find something of this purity, joy, shaming, and unconditional love, in our relationships with babies and young children. We can also perceive it in our interaction with nature, and sometimes especially with animals. Even there, together with the joy of such encounters, we might feel the pain of being exposed by their un-self-conscious purity. The pain of the experience may be one reason why some people abuse children and animals, whose purity and simplicity can show us uncomfortable truths about ourselves.

There's nothing new here. As we hear it in St John's Gospel,

> This is the verdict: Light has come into the world, but people loved darkness instead of light because their deeds were evil. Everyone who does evil hates the light, and will not come into the light for fear that their deeds will be exposed. (Jn 3.19–20, NIV)

But if we can bear that defenselessness and the love and forgiveness that accompanies it, we will gain

. insight into ourselves before God and each other. We will be helped to understand our sin, and begin again on the path towards purity.

Other Ways In

There are, of course, other potential landmarks along the route of our self-discovery as sinners.

One obvious one is **a big failure**. Suddenly we wake up to the realization that by saying something (or not), by taking a course of action (or not), we have done great damage either to ourselves, to someone else, or to the world. The mistake might have taken one second, perhaps when we impulsively press "send" on a really bad e-mail. It might have taken years of festering in a toxic relationship. But suddenly we realize that we have totally blundered, and are filled with regret. Such failures can lead us into vain replayings of our mental tape-loops, about how stupid I sounded when I made that remark about my colleague. But compunction over our serious errors can sometimes serve as a promising lead-in to a more thorough and constructive inventory of our lives.

Another entry can come from contemplating **the fallenness of the world**. We can observe society's subtle failures and mediocrities, or dwell on especially horrible events, and find inklings of those tragedies in the depths of our own hearts. Sometimes we step into a realization that—because we are all so thoroughly interconnected—something exists within each of us that contributes to the disastrous state of affairs. Once in the aftermath of a series of arson attacks against black churches in the South, I was part of an ecumenical committee drafting a prayer service. The other participants mostly proposed prayers that lamented or condemned other people's racism and anger. I suggested a prayer of personal confession, identifying the anger, pettiness, and prejudice that dwell in our own hearts. To which most of the committee replied, "Why? We're not the angry racists. They are." But the ones who took a deeper look inside themselves were markedly uncomfortable with what they saw there. Taking responsibility for the ills of the world can seem like sheer vanity—as if I am personally so consequential!—but it should actually stems from a deep sense that we are all in this together. And wouldn't it seem that our primary duty should be amending our own lives rather than pointing fingers of blame at others? After all, we can take total responsibility for and actually change only ourselves.

A final entry point to consider is **the thought of our mortality**. We're going to die. The older we get, the idea of our death arrives more frequently as the years speed up and our bodies and minds begin failing us more. We may have to confront it after a near-death experience, an accident, a heart attack, preparation for serious surgery, or the purchase of a burial plot. The realization that we will inevitably die has a way of cutting through some of our self-justification. It may even lead to a liberating spontaneity. There's an illustrative moment in, of all places, the musical *Zorba*:

> He said, "I live every minute as if I would never die." Think of that, Boss! He lived as if he would never die. I live as if I would die any minute! For that reason . . . just that reason, I am free!

Traditional ascetical literature encourages us to cultivate the remembrance of our death. *Memento mori*—the recollection that you will die—can lead us to a focused life, doing the things that bring meaning and improvement to people's lives, rather than wasting time on the inconsequential. Imagine the sudden realization that you had just one more day, or one more hour, to live. How would you hurry to prepare yourself? You might seek out pleasurable or meaningful experiences.

But you might instead seek to reconcile yourself with others, with yourself, and with your God. You might take stock of all the ways you've wronged people and seek to set them right. A realization of our mortality will engender a more thoughtful setting of priorities. It should help us ordering our lives so that we minimize harm, quickly seek people's forgiveness, and try to let go of their offenses against us. Our striving in this direction may ultimately prevent us from taking offense at anything, or resenting anyone, because, really, why bother if death is around the corner? *Why bother?*

All of this sounds potentially liberating, doesn't it? Let's contemplate for a moment the incalculable rewards that all of this self-awareness-as-sinner (*forgiven* sinner) can bring. The Church encourages us to pray for the recognition of our sins. During the Canon of Repentance[3] we pray "Give me understanding, O Lord, that I may weep bitterly over my deeds." The reason we want this understanding so much that we pray for it, is that it constitutes true perception of reality. That perception brings inner freedom, compassion, and the freedom from judging others. These are incalculable gifts that we will explore more thoroughly in the next chapter. They amount to an enlightenment that is worth approaching God for and working towards for the whole of our lives.

Some Practical Suggestions

So how do we take the next step on that journey, of the proper discovery of ourselves, of identifying our sinfulness? How do we pursue this gift, without which we are in darkness?

Let me suggest four things:

1) **Pray** for the gift of self-perception—specifically for the gift of the awareness of your own sins, of your particular passions. Asking God to show you the extent of your sin may seem dreadful, dangerous. Can you bear it? Yet you must trust God that he will give you only what you can bear. All your prayer does is indicate to God and yourself your readiness to take a tiny step closer to him. You are stepping infinitesimally closer to an awareness of your brokenness, and your utter contingency upon God and his mercy. "Lord, as you will, as you deem it fit, bring me to an awareness of my sin." If you are ready for a more sustained meditation, read from The Great Canon of St Andrew of Crete, chanted

during Great Lent. Putting us before examples of sinners and saints, it is full of prayers for the recognition of our countless sins, in the sureness of God's loving compassion.

2) **Examine** yourself, consciously. This one is tricky, too, because looking at yourself can become a kind of vainglory. What you might do is examine yourself every day as if you were preparing for confession. I once asked a monk how to prepare for the confession of sins. He advised me to set as a goal to be prepared for confession at every moment of my life. That means if someone were to say, in the middle of my morning coffee or while I'm binge-watching a TV series, "Right now! Here's your chance!" that I'd be totally ready. Think of how it is with your physical health: attention, diagnosis, and healing are most effective when they are ongoing practices, not rare events set aside for once or twice a year. So examine yourself, as a regular discipline. Know and name the passions that you struggle with.[4]

3) As much as you can, **be involved** in the Church's worship life, in its daily, weekly, and

annual rhythms. That would also include observing its cycles of fasting, which are designed to aid in repentance, together with the confession of sins. These disciplines have been tried and tested for ages, guiding us by exposing our vulnerabilities and dependencies. Place yourself consistently within these cycles, ideally without interruption: regularity is important. If you have a bucket of dirty water, and keep a constant, regular drip of pure water, the bucket will gradually become purified. Keep showing up.

4) Put yourself in situations of **purity**, goodness, holiness. Read good books, of all kinds. Put yourself in the presence of good people, especially ones devoted to the pursuit of purity. Learn from time spent with young children and animals, who in their absence of self-consciousness can be profound truth-tellers. Behold beauty and goodness consciously. Expose yourself to their benefits: edification, compunction, tears, love, joy, gratitude.

5) Be alert in times of **crisis.** They may give you particular insight into your shortcomings. The truism that "Our problems are actually opportunities,"

is not an empty one, if you use such challenges
as times to reflect on yourself, remembering too
that you will die.

Whether or not these kinds of suggestions are new
to you, take a moment to consider them. It's a classic
Christian paradox: the greatest saints perceive themselves as the worst sinners. We are always somewhere
along the path of discovering God's greatness and our
own lowliness. There is no time like the present: let
us covenant with ourselves and each other that we
will take the next steps on the journey to our own
self-understanding.

Notes

[1]See Homily 68 , in *The Ascetical Homilies of St. Isaac the Syrian*
(Boston, MA: Holy Transfiguration Monastery, 1984), 334.

[2]*Modern Canterbury Pilgrims*, ed. W. H. Auden and James A.
Pike (New York: Morehouse-Gorham, 1956), 41.

[3]This canon is probably by St Andrew of Crete, though not to be
confused with the Great Canon that is chanted during Great Lent.

[4]We discuss these things later on in this book, in sections on
knowing yourself and naming the passions.

2
Like I Need This?
The Sinner Identity and Its Gifts

How much joy, how much peace of soul would a person have wherever he went . . . if he was one who habitually accused himself . . . that person would have complete freedom from care.

Dorotheos of Gaza[1]

In order to be able to see anything, the eye needs light. In order to see truths about God, ourselves, the world, we require light of another kind. The "enlightenment" of our minds depends on God. As the 20th-century monastic elder Sophrony tells us, "To apprehend sin in oneself is a spiritual act, impossible without grace, without the drawing near to us of divine Light. . . ."[2] Divine Light and the insight that it brings is a matter of gift; it is grace. My access to it doesn't depend entirely on me. I can't will it into existence. For that matter, I can't save myself, I can't have faith purely out of my own intellectual acumen, I can't become virtuous purely out of my own will-power, I can't come to a right understanding of myself and my sinfulness on my own. God grants these gifts.

I have to seek divine Light, and cooperate with it. I have to earnestly desire it. I have to pray about it and pray for it. I have to journey toward actually wanting to perceive myself as sinner. Then I have to work with perceiving myself that way. As St Isaac of Syria writes starkly,

> At once rouse your soul, and with tears persuade him who saves all to draw back the curtain from the door of your heart, to scatter the murk of the passions' storm from your inner sky, and to vouchsafe you to see a ray of daylight, lest you be like one dead, sitting in darkness forever.[3]

He means that we ignore our faults and our passions at our peril. But seeing my true self is painful. Many of us spend a lot of our time and energy avoiding genuine self-discovery. We take refuge in the world's abundant noise, distractions, and mediocrity because even a glimpse of our sins can be horribly unpleasant.

We so often "hate the light . . . lest our deeds should be exposed" (Jn 3.20).

So we may ask, "Why go down that road?" Why petition God for this "gift" of perception if it only shows us our own disease? Since the sinner language and identity can evidently go wrong, why bother with it? Even if as some of what we see in our interior depths isn't pretty, there are benefits to seeing ourselves more clearly. Let's explore some of them.

1. Perception of Reality

Being able to view our faults, passions, misdirected thoughts and deeds unclouds our perception, not just of ourselves, but of everything. To continue the quote by Fr Sophrony above: "True contemplation begins the moment we become aware of sin." True contemplation, that is, of other people, of the created world, and of God—of everything—is contingent upon our awareness of sin in ourselves. We cannot see things as they are if we don't see ourselves as we are.

St John's First Epistle states unequivocally, "If we say we have no sin, we deceive ourselves, and the truth is not in us. . . . If we say we have not sinned, we make [God] a liar, and his word is not in us" (1 Jn 1.8–10).

Our sinfulness is a fact. If we deny that, we are denying God—an overwhelming thought. Perhaps more accessible is the notion that we are deceiving ourselves. Much as we don't want to deny God, we also might be leery of deceiving ourselves. The underlying proposition here is that truth exists, as does falsehood. To propose that I am completely sinless is essentially a guaranteed falsehood, a denial of reality, even in a relativistic and "post-factual" culture.

The claim, then, is that a genuine, uncluttered understanding of other people and of the world around us is predicated on the clearest possible perception of ourselves. This premise operates at many empirical levels, including science. This doesn't mean that every astute scientist is a paragon of personal humility. But good science depends on a realistic assessment of an inquiry's preconceptions and methodological weaknesses. To the extent we are also true to reality, we have a clearer relationship with ourselves, others, and God. And we are then positioned to work to correct our lives.

2. Freedom

I was standing outside a church many years ago when a boy who had just been to confession came out the door. He immediately started running, waving his arms, calling, "I'm flying! I'm flying!" He embodied the purpose of confession, the unburdening of the soul so that it may fly. Would that our every confession of sin had that effect upon us! But we are all familiar with the feeling—sometimes even physiologically—of the lifting of burdens when we have acknowledged a wrong, whether before a friend, a spouse, an authority, or a child. The problems don't necessarily evaporate. There may still be reparative work to do, behavior to change, and feelings to heal. But we can now address these with a clearer conscience, possibly with the committed cooperation of the person we trespassed against.

This dynamic can run very deep. I remember a priest who told me about a stooped, elderly woman who came to him for confession. After it felt like everything was wrapping up, it came to him to ask, "Is there anything, even from a very long time ago, that's on your heart to bring here in confession?" After a long silence, she began sobbing and revealed that she had had an abortion in her youth. She had never before confessed it. The priest, who began weeping with her, somehow managed to convey to her the boundless love of God, whose saints and angels were rejoicing that she had come to this confession. She departed a more upright person, liberated of the burden that she had kept inside herself for so long. She experienced the forgiveness of God and now could begin to forgive herself.

Conscience is powerful. If we know we've done something wrong—we lied, we cheated, we wounded someone with words deliberately—acknowledging that and asking forgiveness may change everything. We can look people in the eye again! Other times, our misdirected thoughts, words, or deeds may be invisible to us. But our conscience causes us to suffer nonetheless. Our ignorance of such sins, our inability to see or articulate them can't shield us from the physical and psychological suffering they cause. Deep inside, they muck up our physical, emotional, spiritual lives.

The liberation of our conscience, through admitting our sins, is linked to a kind of surrender. As we become increasingly aware of our distorted passions, compulsions, addictions, and brokenness, we become increasingly able to yield them to God. We admit our powerlessness over these things and give him charge. We admit the limitations of our own reason and the deceptiveness of our cleverness. We then free ourselves from a slavish obedience to them. What an incredible, unmeasurable relief that is. Because God is limitlessly powerful, good-beyond-good, and endlessly loving.

Oddly enough, some might assume that considering yourself "a sinner" leads to personal weakness, ineffectiveness, and sniveling mousiness. But isn't it the other way around? The people who are most in-touch with themselves tend to be the happiest. They recognize their sins as well as their gifts. They take responsibility for the former and are grateful for the latter, and they work on each. The freest, least self-conscious people are usually those who know full well that they are broken, that they are sinners, and that they depend on a higher power for their very life. That mentality is common to religious ascetics, to recovering addicts (religious or otherwise), and to courageously self-honest people from all walks of life. They know that—left entirely to their own devices—they would be lying in the gutter. Self-knowledge and surrender to God's immeasurable love and strength don't turn you into a church mouse. Quite the opposite: you become fully alive, sure-footed, and truly free.

3. Assurance

This freedom is also liberty from fear. Once we perceive and acknowledge our faults and surrender them to God, we have the deepened assurance of being loved and forgiven. This is not a simple dynamic. Rowan Williams expresses it well in describing the ancient desert monastics:

> The desert fathers and mothers are [. . .] sure that God will forgive, but they know with equal certainty that for us to *receive* that forgiveness in such a way that our lives will be changed is a lifetime's work requiring the most relentless monitoring of our selfish and lazy habits of thinking and reacting.[4]

You may think that, well, everyone desires love, and mercy, and forgiveness. What's not to love about love and mercy? But it is not so simple. Living with and living into another's total love—especially God's—is painfully humbling. Strangely, we may prefer the feeling of being hated to the exposed and shameful feeling of being totally loved. It is indeed a lifetime's work to receive God's love and forgiveness. But even as we undertake that work, we are already experiencing the "blessed assurance" that God has saved the world, and that God loves and saves even me. To the extent that I have made an inventory of myself and submitted it to the loving God, I no longer obsess over what people think of me, whether others esteem me. Whether people treat me like gold or like dirt, I will always recall that I am known and loved, and that my life is taken up in the living God. I can walk sure-footedly, confident, fully alive. In God.

Williams writes further about the ancient desert ascetics: "They know with utter seriousness the cost to them of their sin and selfishness and vanity, yet know that God will heal and accept." Divine acceptance doesn't soften the intensity with which they know their sinfulness. But it has implications for relationships with other people, as "their knowledge of [their sins] is what gives them their almost shocking tenderness towards other sinners."[5]

4. Non-Judgment

"People who live in glass houses shouldn't throw stones." This old adage points out that if I am aware of the depth of my vulnerability and weakness—my glass house—I will be less likely to denounce others. After all, as we sometimes say casually, "Who am I to judge?" Or more seriously, "How can I condemn someone else when I myself do worse?"

This can be taken to extremes. I once went to confession to a priest who, at every wrongdoing that I mentioned, would say, "Don't worry, I do that too!" A sweet and kind person, maybe his pastoral sensibilities dictated that this was what I needed to hear in the moment, as a comfort. But in principle his good nature misapplied the sin/confession dynamic. The commandment not to judge any person (Mt 7.1; Rom 2.1, etc.) doesn't mean that we should not call out sin for what it is, in ourselves and in others. This is true especially if we're in the role of hearing out people's faults and helping guide them. We are supposed to discern sin as part of a genuine perception of reality. Sin exists. Evil exists. When someone does evil, it may be entirely appropriate to hold them responsible. But we are not to judge the person, or worse, condemn the person—only the actions. We cannot claim to know the inner reality that compelled them to act wrongly. Friend or foe, we can only entrust them to the loving, merciful God: "God loves your enemies as much as he loves you."[6]

We are supposed to be occupied exclusively with our own sin, to the extent that we rightly condemn ourselves. But self-condemnation is not self-hatred. It means seeing ourselves as unworthy of salvation or, in other words, dependent entirely on God's mercy. But condemning *others* as unworthy of God's salvation is wrong. The extent to which we are aware of our own depravity, contrasted with God's holiness and mercy, is the extent to which it becomes unthinkable for us to stand in judgment of another person.

Some of the great Christian writers warn against censuring others. St Dorotheos of Gaza writes, "It is part of humility to scrutinize severely one's own wrong-doing and to be sympathetic and forbearing towards one's neighbor,"[7] citing two sides of the spiritual coin. Fr Seraphim Rose, a stern monastic of the 20th century, writes in one of his letters of spiritual guidance, "Don't criticize or judge other people—regard everyone else as an angel, justify their mistakes and weaknesses, and condemn only yourself as the worst sinner."[8] There is thus an inextricable connection between knowing one's own faults and the refusal or even inability to judge another person. One ascetic, Moses the Black, put it in terms of time management: "If one is carrying his [own] sins he does not see his neighbor's."[9] Another wrote about the absurdity of disparaging others' messiness when your own house is disordered: "If you want to find repose both here and there, say in every situation: 'I, who am I?' and do not pass judgment on anybody."[10] But the connection becomes something still deeper than non-judgment. It has to do with the softening of your heart, remaining open to the other. It has to do with compassion.

5. Compassion

We should not judge others. If we see ourselves as we are, we will find it simply impossible to. Self-understanding yields mercy, empathy, tolerance, love of the other. St Seraphim of Sarov, who lived at the turn of the 19th century, observed, "We condemn others only because we shun knowing ourselves." Our deepening realization of our own sin coupled with our increasing experience of God's mercy will fill us with compassion for others. We will begin to realize that no one is beyond redemption. We will rejoice in people's small and great acts of kindness. We will cheer their successes. We will experience empathetic sorrow at their struggles and failings. We will not pretend to know or fully understand the intricacies of the internal and external factors in their hearts. We will fervently wish for them nothing but God's abundant grace, blessing, and love. We will pray that they increasingly come to a conscious knowledge of that love.

* * *

Living in reality, free and fearless, judging no one, with true compassion towards all, even as you work toward the correction of your life—these are the repercussions of a healthy knowledge of yourself, realistically acknowledge your sins and your total dependency on our loving God. These are gifts, which may give you an inkling of why it might be worth embarking on the journey to seeing yourself as a sinner. We will hear more about them in the pages to come.

Notes

[1]Dorotheus of Gaza, *Dorotheos of Gaza: Discourses and Sayings* (Kalamazoo, MI: Cistercian Publications, 1977), 141. St Dorotheus refers this teaching to Abba Poemen.

[2]Archimandrite Sophrony, *His Life is Mine*, 41.

[3]Homily 68. REFERENCE?

[4]*Silence and Honey Cakes: The Wisdom of the Desert* (Oxford: Lion Hudson, 2003), 35.

[5]Ibid., 36.

[6]See "Mother Gavrilia: All-Pervading Love for Everyone," *The Wheel* 9/10 (2017): 56.

[7]Dorotheos of Gaza, *Discourses and Sayings*, 161.

[8]Reproduced two years after Fr Seraphim's death, in the Jan.-Feb. 1984 issue of the journal *Living Orthodoxy.*

[9]Moses the Black, Saying 16 (Moses to Poemen 3), in *Give Me a Word: The Alphabetical Sayings of the Desert Fathers*, trans. John Wortley, Popular Patristics Series 52 (Yonkers, NY: St Vladimir's Seminary Press, 2014), 197.

[10]Joseph of Panepho, Saying 2, in *Give Me a Word*, 150.

3
Am I Really the Worst?

*Spare even me, though by defying your commands
I am the worst sinner in the world.*

Great Canon of St Andrew of Crete

*I believe, O Lord . . . that you are the Christ, the Son
of the Living God, who came into the world to save
sinners, of whom I am the first.*

Prayers said before Holy Communion
(attributed to St John Chrysostom)

S t Paul, one of the Church's greatest saints, writes "I
am the foremost of sinners" (1 Tim 1.15). Before
he became "St Paul," indeed before he even became
"Paul," he was "Saul," who hunted down, persecuted,
and killed Christians. So, you might be tempted to
say, "Well, maybe he actually *was* the worst!" But he
doesn't write in the past tense that "I *was* the foremost

of sinners." He makes his statement in the present tense. The saint who sailed from city to city to preach of Christ and lay the foundations of the Church through his letters, along the way getting shipwrecked, publicly whipped, and imprisoned, considers himself the chief of transgressors. We find this pattern throughout Christian history: the greatest of our saints consider themselves the worst of sinners.

But the Church invites each and every one of us to think of ourselves as the lowest of sinners. Which is obviously illogical. How can each of us be the worst? It's just as unreasonable as thinking each can be the best. If the playing field is level, the ranks of "worst" or "best" are meaningless.

Furthermore, isn't it potentially prideful to boast, even to yourself, that you are the worst? Especially if we equate awareness of sinfulness with virtue, well, what happens when you call yourself the worst? Doesn't that effectively make you the best? Can you really blame the whole world's malaise on your transgressions? Take a deep breath: your sins are likely not so remarkable. They're probably quite banal.

"I am the foremost of sinners." How can I make sense of this statement as I strive to make it my own? To date, I haven't launched any genocides. I haven't physically tortured or murdered anyone. Surely there are worse sinners than me.

All fair enough. But this superlatively dire self-assessment is also entirely right in several critically important ways.

For one, to the best of my knowledge, it is actually true. I can't fully know the misdeeds, circumstances, external strictures, inner struggles, or repentance of other people. It is not mine to analyze other people's shortcomings or their motivations. Doing so will not benefit me. Plus, their failings are fully known only to God. I have access to and control over only myself. I can bring only myself before God's judgment. And I will tell you that the picture is not very pretty. Given the circumstances in which I was raised, my education and life in the Church, what I have seen and what I know, for me to harbor the kind of thoughts I have, to speak the words I say, and do the deeds I do is utterly inexcusable. As for the state of my repentance? The quality of my prayer? Forget it. I can't say how it goes for anyone else. I honestly have no idea. But there's a really good chance they are doing this all better than I do, thanks be to God.

I don't know the hearts of others, but I do know something of my heart. So I suspect that, if I were actually in a position of totalitarian control and found myself threatened, who knows the evils I might commit? While I was living in Japan in the 1980s, I visited Hiroshima. I spent hours wandering through the memorials and exhibits that recount the events and aftermath of August 6, 1945, when the US dropped an atom bomb on the city in one of the last events of World War II. I came across a life-sized replica of the bomb that laid waste to the city and destroyed hundreds of thousands of lives. As I looked at that murderous piece of metal, I had a sudden, momentary vision of that bomb, in a tiny form, inside my own heart. I saw this specter as a gift from God, a fledgling insight that there is no sin that I am not capable of doing or rationalizing. There is no sin that I am not capable of committing within the recesses of my heart or potentially in reality. It is still hard for me to say, with complete commitment, that I am the foremost of all sinners. But I know how it is possible to say it and mean it.

The Door to Mercy

Recognizing ourselves as the lowest of all opens us to God's mercy. As St Paul writes,

The grace of our Lord overflowed for me with the faith and love that are in Christ Jesus. The saying is sure and worthy of full acceptance, that Christ Jesus came into the world to save sinners, of whom I am the foremost. But I received mercy for this reason, that in me, as the foremost, Jesus Christ might display his perfect patience as an example to those who were to believe in him for eternal life. (1 Tim 1.14–16)

We are sinners surrounded by sinners. The paragraph above follows a catalogue of "murderers of fathers and murderers of mothers, for manslayers, sexually immoral persons, kidnapers, liars . . ." (vv. 9–10). But this human condition, in all its depravity, is what Christ came to save. St Paul, identifying himself as worse even than the manslayers and "sodomites," sets himself up as the paradigm of God's mercy and forbearance with people. St Paul seems to be saying, "If God is patient with me—the worst of the lot—then we have to believe he will be merciful to everyone. If someone like me can be saved, then there's hope for us all."

I wrote in an earlier chapter that an awareness of the world's brokenness may lead to the realization that I myself play a consequential role in that brokenness.

It's easy to follow this idea down the wrong path. For example, I might delude myself into thinking I am personally the most important factor in the world's destiny. Better that it create in me a sense of my own responsibility before the world, which can lead me through faith in God into holiness of life, peace of soul, and joy of heart. Dostoevsky captures this concept in *The Brothers Karamazov,* when the Elder Zosima recounts a conversation between his dying brother Markel and his mother:

> "[I] tell you, dear mother, that each of us is guilty in everything before everyone, and I most of all."
> . . . "How can it be . . . that you are the most guilty before everyone? There are murderers and robbers, and how have you managed to sin so that you should accuse yourself most of all?" "Dear mother, heart of my heart . . . you must know that verily each of us is guilty before everyone, for everyone and everything! I do not know how to explain it to you, but I feel it so strongly that it pains me. And how could we have lived before, getting angry, and not knowing anything?" Thus he awoke every day with more and more tenderness, rejoicing and all atremble with love.[1]

Imminent death sharpens Markel's self-understanding, before God and the world. He acutely perceives the fall of humanity and his own particular place within this total picture. In this, Markel also perceives the deep interconnectivity of all people and things. The dividing line between himself and "the other" is being erased. In this way, his perception of his deep fallenness brings him neither maudlin wailing, nor pathos, nor self-loathing. Instead he experiences joy, compassion, and love. Having come to this awareness, he can't comprehend how he ever lost his temper with anyone. The call to understand ourselves as "chief of sinners" entails making a practice of understanding ourselves the way Markel does. Staretz Sophrony (Sakharov), one of the great spiritual elders of our age, used to say that when anyone sought his spiritual counsel or confession, he would in his heart locate himself beneath that person in his spiritual stature. His counsel to others was therefore imbued with genuine humility, which in turn creates clarity of perception. It also leads to saying less, rather than more, another habit the ascetics recommend as a matter of course.

Placing ourselves beneath everyone, whatever their deeds, demeanor, or status in life is of course a challenge. But it is feasible. It does not entail allowing ourselves to get walked over, treated unfairly, or cheated. Just because I'm a worse sinner than my plumber doesn't mean he gets to overcharge me, or install leaky pipes. Being "lower" than my employees does not mitigate their accountability to me. Putting myself spiritually beneath my boss does not entail that I surrender my prerogative to being treated and compensated fairly. It does mean, though, that I am able to say that my plumber, employees, and boss will be in heaven ahead of me.

It behooves us, in all this, to recall that self-knowledge, and even self-abasement before others, are not a destination that we ever fully attain. They are something to be constantly sought. Nor are they ends in themselves, but a means to a genuine and liberating humility. The process is in no way automatic. In fact, it is something of a mystery. Dorotheos of Gaza sums the matter up perfectly:,

> Seeking to know oneself and to put oneself below everyone else and praying to God about everything: this is the road to humility, but humility itself is something divine and incomprehensible.[2]

As we have observed, seeing ourselves as sinners, the worst of sinners, can be neurotic, destructive, or prideful; or it can be part of our journey towards enlightenment in God, part of our receiving his mercy. We have seen above, and in the previous chapter, the barometers of a healthy and true self-perception: an increase in compassion, mercy, love, and the inconceivability of judging others.

As St Dorotheos has reminded us, attaining that sensibility of genuine, consistent humility is both a divine gift and a human process. Neither is fully comprehensible to us, as if it were an assembly manual. It is a matter of seeking. We may pray to God, to grant us greater humility, in the ability to see ourselves as *less worthy than anyone else*. This may be a frightening prayer to speak, because such lessons are often taught us by means of challenge; humility often comes through humiliation. Or sometimes, more refreshingly, by a surprising revelation about someone we had always thought to be a bad person, showing her in fact to be capable of sheer selfless compassion.

Our prayer for humility therefore is both a sign and a builder of an *inner readiness* to be shown such truths, about ourselves and about others whom we judge. May God reveal to us these truths, as he wishes, and in such time as he discerns that we are able to receive them.

Notes

[1]Fyodor Dostoevsky, *The Brothers Karamazov*, trans. Richard Pevear and Larissa Volokhonsky (New York: Quartet, 1990), 289.

[2]*Discourses and Sayings*, p. 101.

4
Reflections on the Self

"Take pains to enter your innermost chamber and you will see the chamber of heaven, for they are one and the same, and in entering one you behold them both."

Tito Colliander[1]

"My testimony is valid because I know where I have come from and where I am going."

John 8.14

"Enter into yourself, dwell within your heart, for God is there."

Ephrem the Syrian[2]

We've been discussing recognizing ourselves as sinners, seeing this as a gift that God gives for our enlightenment and our emancipation. This recognition is a process, perpetually growing in understanding ourselves and how we relate to God and the world. We now need to look more comprehensively at the implications of the discovery of self. Self-knowledge has long been considered a virtue. In the sixth century BC, "Know thyself" was inscribed on the Temple of Apollo at Delphi, in Greece. But our conception of "the self" has changed over the centuries. In this chapter, we will talk about coming to know it as we define it today, naming it, and wrestling with it.

Self-Knowledge

There has been a great deal of attention paid to the self at all levels of contemporary society. The advent of psychoanalysis in the 20th century spawned a new interest in and respect for the practice of a person's internal exploration, and has evolved through diverse schools of psychology and psychiatry.

As a part of self-exploration, the 20th century also got people thinking in new ways about collective identities, such as those related to nationality, gender, race, socioeconomics, and others. What does it mean to be a man or a woman? A member of the middle class in North America? How does the color of your skin affect your place in the world? The matrix of all these different sub-distinctions has led to the idea that identity itself is a cultural construct. That is, identity as such doesn't biologically exist. We ourselves, and those in our surroundings (either with us or against us) invent and shape it. So we can speak of a "self," but the characteristics by which that self is known are arbitrary and therefore malleable.

The fundamental insight that we play a role in constructing our identity can be helpful in our exploration of self. Putting a stop to the habitual negatives we may bombard ourselves with that help form our sense of ourselves ("I stink at math," "I'm too fat") can release us from artificial limitations. But beware of concluding that the self or identity does not exist. Christian tradition has it that God has bestowed on each of us a unique self, an identity, a name. That is one reason that our forebears in the Church place such great stock on the knowledge of the self.

Take St Basil the Great, the fourth-century spiritual giant from Caesarea in Asia Minor. The "self" in his day wasn't considered a construct. In a homily called "Take Heed to Yourself,"[3] St Basil doesn't tell people to "think of themselves in new ways." He doesn't tell them to "transcend stereotypes about class and gender." Instead he describes the practical benefits and spiritual importance of self-knowledge. Those benefits include healthier relationships and a right life, he writes, but true knowledge of self leads to something far greater: access to the knowledge of God.

So, we may ask, how do you come to know your inner self? St Basil is realistic about the limits of what we can learn. A significant part of his career as a theologian was devoted to arguing against people who believed that God was perfectly comprehensible. His theological insight had shown that idea to be outrageous. Aetius of Antioch, a follower of the Arian heresy, had written: "I know God with such perfect clarity and I understand and know him to such a degree, that I understand God better than I understand myself."[4] To which St Basil replied, "I do not even know myself! How can I presume to know the unknowable God?" Both viewpoints suggest that knowing ourselves is somehow related to knowing God. St Basil, however, rightly sees that we can attain only partial apprehension of *either*.

How, then, do we come to an even partial knowledge of God? By his "energies," says St Basil (or "activities," from the Greek *energeia*).[5] In other words, we know who God is by what God does. We can apply the same principle to ourselves. By which I mean that knowing ourselves is likewise achieved partly through perceiving our own "energies": we learn about ourselves by observing what we do, what we want—from our actions, our deeds, our will.

What does that mean practically? In many ways, knowing yourself is like knowing anything. A lot of it comes naturally, just by living an increasing number of days. Some might be deliberate and cultivated, in the sense that you might make a conscious decision to study your inner patterns and tendencies. Some might involve discussing your impressions with a trusted adviser. Different kinds of insights, perhaps overlapping, may come from intentional (and possibly confessional) conversations with a friend, a spiritual father/mother, a psychologist, a psychiatrist, or even a child. I wouldn't necessarily place these all on a par with each other. But each in its way has the potential to yield powerful insight. "Advisors" to avoid are those who claim spiritual or psychic powers, especially through Tarot, crystals, or other such means, as their insights may be deceitful, even demonic.

Here we should return to this book's main theme. A searching reflection on ourselves will result in many observations, one of which, inevitably, is that we sin. We think, say, and do things that are contrary to the God whom we claim to know and love. We think and act contrary to God's way and to his law. It is hard to imagine that we might emerge from a probing self-reflection saying, "You know, I'm actually sinless! I've fulfilled every commandment, and my heart is always set upon God, and I have never grieved anyone." Narcissists are liable to think like this. One of Jesus's inquirers, more likely naïve than narcissistic, tells Jesus that, yes he has fulfilled the commandments: "Teacher, all these I have observed from my youth" (Mk 10.20). How does Jesus react? He looks at him and loves him (v. 21). Then he raises the criteria substantially (and here I paraphrase): You think you are sinless because you didn't kill anyone or sleep with your neighbor? That's a good start. Now you have to have to detach yourself from your riches. You have to consider other people and even devote your life to them, especially the poor.

Virtually nobody with a healthy psyche can truthfully say, on reflection, "I have always done well by God and by neighbor." Genuine self-examination will show how we sin and fall short of the glory of God. We are sinners. Naming that fact and owning that identity are indispensable to our spiritual journey. Now it is time to ask some legitimate questions about naming ourselves "sinners." I may understand that "I am a sinner" is a true statement. But could it also potentially be harmful?

The Power of Naming

One question on that score has to do with the power of the name. There are many different ways of naming. There are common names we give people (Peter, Patricia, Michael, Elizabeth), as well as designations we bestow according to function (teacher, musician, plumber), to condition or state (cancer patient, alcoholic, army veteran) or to perceived behavior or status (savior, liar, fool, renaissance man). When we identify someone, in any of these different ways, we may be doing two things. On the one hand, we are identifying an evident reality—someone is a professional, a mother, a schizophrenic, maybe all these at once. But in many cases, we are *pre*scribing a reality, for good or for ill. I recall how, once I started naming or identifying myself as a musician, I felt empowered to create music with greater purpose. But what about the kid whose parents constantly identified her as "bad at sports" and "good at math"? Perhaps these qualities were demonstrable by her grades, but as these became part of her identity, they would increasingly *shape* her reality. So what does it mean, in this context, for me to identify myself as a sinner? Would that—should that—contribute to the shaping of my reality? Recognizing myself as a "musician" licensed and encouraged me to flourish artistically, so would recognizing myself as a "sinner" license me to sin with greater purpose and élan?

Naming things is a way of expressing a certain authority over them. When God gives Adam charge to name all the animals, he is also conferring on the human person the stewardship of the natural world (Gen 2.19). It is a powerful thing: when we name someone or something, we are helping to shape its destiny. Jesus names Peter to express his destiny of being the rock (*petros*) on which the Church would be built (Mt 16.18). God sees fit to change people's names in order to reflect changes in their functions/destinies: Abram becomes Abraham, Saul becomes Paul. Jesus, which means "God saves" is "the name by which we are saved,"[6] and each of the many appellations by which Jesus is known (Lord, Door, Redeemer, Peace) has a precise meaning, indicating aspects of his identity as savior.[7]

Think for a moment of how we name our children and the ways this might affect our perception of them. We might baptize our child after a saint, family member, or important friend. Some of us christen our children for significant historical or cultural figures; some may even tag them with aspirational qualities, such as Justice, Felicity, or Serena. But how we name them will not only reflect but also affect our relationship with them.[8]

The capacity of personal names both to identify and to shape reality carries over into the other words that we use to describe ourselves. Such as "sinner." What effect does that "name" have on me? Let's imagine that during the formative years of my life, my family regularly referred to me as a mistake. What if my parents hit me or assaulted me and blamed me for their actions? What if I have been systematically degraded in my society because of my skin color, gender, or social status? If that is my context, then designating myself as a sinner (or one of its variants, such as "a wretch") could potentially feed into harmful, self-destructive tendencies that I have already established. However, within the total context of the Church, and the deep-level healing and love it ideally embodies, the epithet "sinner" can play a crucial part in the healing of my memories of abuse and in my coming clean. This is complex stuff, and if you do find myself in this situation, it is imperative to seek out the guidance of a wise, compassionate, and experienced spiritual guide, as not every confessor is qualified to help.

But even for those who do not carry such painful associations, the wider question remains. If I dub myself a sinner, am I giving that word a power over myself? Am I in danger of letting "sinner" become entwined with my truest self? Does the identity of entrap me into transgressive behavior by enshrining it?

These questions lead us to reflect further on the different kinds of power that names have. Because, despite all we've said thus far on the subject, labels do not necessarily determine us. Rather than dictating our behavior, the words we use to describe ourselves can instead be the basis of greater self-understanding and, therefore, of positive transformation. Using personality tests can help us find ways to describe our traits in ways that can be helpful. The Meyers-Briggs is one such. Like others of its type, it may not deliver a stunning epiphany—and remember that some call these kinds of tests into question—but many people have gained insights through them. Such tests are liable to tell you about tendencies in how you take decisions, think through problems, react to the company of others, and interact with the world. "Naming" such things can help us to treat other people—and ourselves—in a more realistic and perhaps more forgiving way. They helped me understand some basic things about myself, such as the fact that engaging in small talk can make my skin crawl isn't because I hate other people but because I'm something of an introvert. I can now observe myself more dispassionately in these circumstances, knowing that this is part of how I'm wired. And I can work with that wiring to find ways of adapting my thoughts and behavior that are realistic and compassionate but still create the spiritual and other changes that I hope for.

Whatever the diagnostic methods we use, we must beware of feeling trapped by our newly discovered identity markers: sensitive or intuitive, judging or perceptive, a "thinking" or "feeling" decision-maker. We can draw insight from such tests as appropriate. They point to tendencies that we can live with or transcend. But to work with them in your journey requires first identifying them.

The necessity of naming a condition is all the more important when it is a malady. In order to heal a sickness, you have to diagnose it, so that you can understand it in its context. In order to transcend a condition, you have to recognize it. That principle very much applies to the condition that we name as sinner. Transcending sin begins with identifying it. Name the sin:

claim it. Now, work on it: confess it. Repent. Surrender it to God on your own as well as in community with other transgressors.

One place that you can see these recommendations carried out is within the world of addiction. It's not that addiction is a sin in itself. Rather, it is a powerful example of the importance of naming a condition in order to help heal it. For example, in the 12-step world one of the first steps in the treatment of addiction involves openly calling yourself an addict. As you begin your recovery, and at every subsequent meeting, you stand up to say, "I am an alcoholic." "I am a drug addict." "I have a gambling problem." You might wonder are they giving such identities too much power, letting them shape their behavior? As in, "If I'm an alcoholic, then drinking is what I do, so . . . pour me a drink!"

Yes, an alcoholic or any other addict in these circumstances is surrendering to that as part of his or her identity. But the right kind of surrender is a powerful step toward recovery. Meletios Webber, an Orthodox author, weighs in on this aspect of the 12 steps:

> The statement "I am an alcoholic," is packed with meaning. . . . It means, "I admit I have a problem." Any alcoholic who can say that is separated from

the countless numbers of alcoholics who go to their graves rather than admit they have a problem.[9]

Substitute "I am a sinner" and you can see that it, too, means "I have a problem." It does not define the totality of who you are. You are admitting that you are not whole. That you have a problem. Webber continues:

> The statement "I am an alcoholic" means, "I am not God," or even, "I am not God, [and therefore] someone else must be." In turn, since someone else is God, the drinker is free to let [God] do his job. The alcoholic is then free to be himself, and to find and settle into whatever the real God may have in store for him.

Likewise, "I am a sinner" means that you have lost command of yourself and you on your own cannot regain it. You must submit to God, who is in control. Understood this way, saying "I am a sinner" means, "God, your will be done." Lastly, Webber writes, "The title 'alcoholic' is worn as a badge of honor, and it gives the bearer a sense of belonging in a group where everyone bears that title." Translating that into the language of "sinner," we understand ourselves as sinners-in-community, being redeemed in the communion of the Church.

If we take the 12-step model as our guide, then, we can say that calling ourselves "sinners" is part of acknowledging the problem, submitting to God, and our badge as a member of the Church, the hospital for transgressors. All of us in the Church are. We have to accomplish both by ourselves and together with each other our way forward in Christ toward freedom from sin.

So "sinner" is not a trap but a surrender and there-fore—paradoxically—a liberation. It admits brokenness and yields power to God. It signals membership in a community that is the Body of Christ even as it is also constantly becoming that Body through healing faults, mending brokenness, and restoring the divine image. The community comprises broken persons who know that their wholeness rests entirely in Christ and depends entirely on God. I mentioned earlier that recovering addicts (especially those in recovery programs), church-goers or not, often understand the whole "forgiven sinner" dynamic so well, precisely because they acutely recognize their brokenness and powerlessness, so they surrender those to their Higher Power even as they con-tinue to work on themselves. They are in the business of learning about and being honest with themselves, each other, and their Higher Power. They get it, much better than many of us righteous church-folk.

So if naming is power, it isn't absolute power. I noted above the importance of God's assigning Adam to name the animals. It spoke to human stewardship and authority over the animal world. Properly understood, that authority is realized and exercised in humility. The earth is the Lord's and the fullness thereof belongs to God (Ps 24.1). Ultimately, nothing is mine to own and abuse. Creation exists to praise and serve God. I have to exercise and direct my stewardship with that in mind in order to bring the animals into creation's praise of the Lord. I can treat my passions likewise. I can name them, take responsibility for them, and strive to direct them according to God's will. So it is with my transgression. I recognize it for what it is and submit so my weakness can be brought to his service.

Once I have managed to do that, calling myself "sinner" can turn into an immense relief. I begin to feel the weight being lifted from my chest. I have begun my surrender to God. I have surrendered a control that I could not realistically hope to maintain. I am allowing God to be God, giving him space to do his work, in me. I am doing so through the Church, the community of other sinners being healed in Christ. It is a consolation and a relief to know that sin has been defeated and will ultimately be forgiven by the merciful God.

So let's name ourselves sinners, together, remembering that our brokenness may be the key to bringing God into our lives.

Identifying My Self—or Selves?

The purpose of understanding and even naming myself as a sinner is twofold. It lets me tell the truth about myself in relationship to God and others. It also frees me to acknowledge my need for healing and my surrender to God, as I continue to pursue purity and holiness.

But having established the benefits of acknowledging ourselves as sinners, we need to ask again: Does "sinner" define the totality of who I am? Is my particular self innately depraved? If it is, is that why the ascetical literature recommends fleeing self-love or despising myself?

At the very least, I have to reconcile those questions and that advice with the conviction that this very substance of mine is made in God's image. Should I not then consider myself truly good and beautiful? If so, should I not rather love and rejoice in myself?

Or is it that I am somehow composed of two selves, a sinful one to be denied and hated, and a God's-image-bearing self that needs to be encouraged and loved? Are there parts of myself to love, cherish, and be true to, and parts to be ignored, denied, hated . . . even died to? Further, are these my only two components, or are there more? In which case, *how many people am I?* (The hackneyed advice to "be yourself" was challenged in the Pixar film *The Incredibles*, where a frustrated fanboy named Buddy addresses his hero: "You always say 'Be true to yourself.' But you never say which part of yourself to be true to!" The personality, as Buddy realizes, is not a simple monolith.)

St Paul also faced the conundrum of conflicting parts of himself in a stirring confession in his Epistle to the Romans:

> I do not understand my own actions. For I do not do what I want, but I do the very thing I hate. . . . But in fact it is no longer I that do it, but sin that dwells within me.

Virtually all of us can empathize with his inner conflict. Who of us hasn't said, "I know the right thing to do, but I don't do it. It almost feels like there's something foreign living in me." St Paul continues his lament:

I can will what is right, but I cannot do it. For I do not do the good I want, but the evil I do not want is what I do. Now if I do what I do not want, it is no longer I that do it, but sin that dwells within me.[10]

He sees sin as a force, sort of like we view a virus. In pursuing the idea, he recognizes a pattern in his thoughts and actions:

So I find it to be a law that when I want to do what is good, evil lies close at hand. For I delight in the law of God in my inmost self, but I see in my members another law at war with the law of my mind, making me captive to the law of sin that dwells in my members.

Crucially, even as he admits that his actions betray him, he professes that he has *an innermost self* that is still capable of delight in the divine commandments. Brothers and sisters, all is not lost. Like St Paul, our inmost self also delights in God and his statutes. Our inmost self is good and true. We are not totally depraved. But we are deeply confused. And sin is there to confuse us.

Finally, we see that although St Paul is exasperated with himself, he never doubts his salvation through the Messiah:

Wretched man that I am! Who will rescue me from this body of death? [What is the solution?] Thanks be to God through Jesus Christ our Lord! . . . There is therefore now no condemnation for those who are in Christ Jesus. For the law of the Spirit of life in Christ Jesus has set you free from the law of sin and of death.

Christ has set us free! It is finished. It is consummated. As fraught as this inner wrestling can be, Christ enters this whole broken dynamic, taking it to its furthest point, all the way to *death,* and he transcends and transforms it so that it no longer has the grip on us that it once had. How vital this is to recall, and how easy it is to forget.

So it is important to grasp that Christ has set me free. But I must remember that I nevertheless remain confused. I must keep both of these realities in mind concurrently. As St Silouan of Mount Athos learned from the Lord: "Keep your mind in hell"—recalling your state of degradation—but at the same time "Despair not,"[11] for you know that Christ has won this victory for you, for us all. Because of Christ, we are not enslaved to sin.

But let's return to consider St Paul's "innermost self." We all have one, our most true self. It is good and delights in God who made it in his image. The 19th-century presbyter St John of Kronstadt once wrote:

> Never confuse the person, formed in the image of God, with the evil that is in him, because evil is but a chance misfortune, illness, a devilish reverie. But the very essence of the person is the image of God, and this remains in him despite every disfigurement.[12]

In the 20th century, in a sermon on the parable of the Publican and the Pharisee, St Nikolai (Velimirovich) of Zicha preached about a person's inner essence contrasted with the wrong kind of self-love—or the love of "the wrong self," as it were.

> When a person loves only himself, he loves neither God nor his fellow-men. He does not even love the person that is in himself; he loves only his thoughts about himself, his illusions about himself. Were he to love the person in himself, he would love God's image in him, and would quickly become a lover of God and man, for he would be seeking man and God in other people, as objects of his love.[13]

The Pharisee openly praises himself, even "prays with himself" (Lk 18.11). St Nikolai shows how the Pharisee's admiration of his own thoughts and illusions about himself set a loathsome example. If you were to follow suit, you would come to hate God and your fellow people. St Nikolai advises, instead, to love the actual person in ourselves so that we can come to love God and other people. That true inner person, or inmost self, is what St Paul calls "the inside" or "inner self" (2 Cor 4.16), as opposed to "the flesh."

So it is that, at heart, I am a good and precious person. Even so, I apprehend that I am fallen and, as such, I can't be trusted. *I cannot be trusted.* Left to my own devices, my self-will, my passions, I would indeed be lost. I would be a danger to myself and to others and a shame before God.

* * *

Now, all of this still might sound as if we suffer from multiple personality disorder. Do we have two selves, an inner to love and an outer to hate? No—what we have is one innermost self that is broken by sin. That sin, these foibles and passions, are not a second self; they are the dirt on the mirror. The Orthodox funeral service reminds us of our real identity when we sing, "I am the image of your ineffable glory, though I bear the brands of transgressions."

We are, in our true selves, mirrors of the divine. But the glass is dirty, even bent. Not surprisingly, this comes to the fore in church services in Great Lent. During the penitential Canon of St Andrew of Crete, which in many churches inaugurates the Lenten Fast, we sing:

> O Savior, I have defiled the garment of my flesh
> and polluted that which you fashioned within
>   me
> according to your own image and likeness.[14]

I have sullied that which resembles the Lord in me by my choices, the things I have allowed myself to think, say, and do. Because of sin that lives in me. Because of evil.

Generally we don't like to dwell on evil or the devil because, if we become obsessed with the devil, he wins. He also wins, however, if we try to ignore the power that evil has over us. All of us. Even St Paul, the great apostle, who was caught up in the third heaven (2 Cor 12.2), was subject to the force of immorality. Even though Christ has set us free from sin, it continues to exert powerful influence on us.

Who am I? This human being, made in the image and glory of God, greater even than the angels, is the same person who gives in to evil, defiling the universe with impure thoughts and shameful deeds. I am a single, beautiful-but-broken self. My freedom in Christ begins by acknowledging this very paradox.

Epilogue

St Paul's passage about his Jekyll-and-Hyde inner struggles ("For I do not do the good I want, but the evil I do not want is what I do") closes with a clear sense of who and what his deepest self really is, in God's love. Which is also how he regards his audience. Toward the end of the same letter, he expresses his wishes for the community: "May the God of hope fill you with all joy and peace in believing, so that you may abound in hope by the power of the Holy Spirit." He acknowledges their true inner selves: "I myself feel confident about you, my brothers and sisters, that you yourselves are full of goodness, filled with all knowledge, and able to instruct one another."[15] Paul is well aware of bickering and dissent within the churches. Many of his letters, after all, were written to quell their arguments. He knows what human beings are made of. He also knows the power of Christ and the Holy Spirit, and how they operate in the community. The final words of his letter to the Romans, however, are not about sin, darkness, or delusion. That's because when people make themselves aware of their hold over us—and Christ's dominion over them—what's left is hope, joy, and peace.

* * *

This chapter covered a lot of concepts. Essentially it was about knowing ourselves realistically and honestly. We saw that it's possible to identify ourselves in limiting ways ("I'm unattractive" or "I'm inept"). But a realistic naming of ourselves as sinners, as sufferers of particular passions and compulsions, is vital to being healed. Despite an apparent split between our good self and our bad self, what lies at our core is an essential goodness, patterned on ineffable divine goodness.

Self-knowledge arrives with time, with age. It comes by paying attention, seeking patterns, scrutinizing the inner impulses that lead to our thoughts, words, and actions. Though much of that work is interior, it also benefits from discussion, perhaps with an experienced counselor, a spiritual director, or a friend. It can happen especially fully and fruitfully within the context of the Church. To that end, it is good to be attentive to its penitential and festal rhythms, and to the texts of its prayers. But we must strive for balance, avoiding both vain self-obsession as well as merely skimming the surface. The key, really, is radical but realistic honesty with ourselves.

Since knowing yourself involves studying what you do, what you think, what you want, many of us find it helpful to keep a journal. The discipline of writing a daily chronicle of your actions, thoughts, and realizations— sometimes shorter, sometimes longer, sometimes insightful and sometimes totally banal—can be part of a program of mindfulness and self-understanding.

As with all of the endeavors within this book, self-knowledge is a gift as much as a process. Pray about it and for it:

O Lord, in your time and as you will, open to me the mystery of my innermost self, created in your Holy Image. Teach me too about the tendencies in me that distort that self. May my self-reflection be neither vain nor perfunctory. May it orient me all the more to your glory.

Notes

[1]Tito Colliander, *The Way of the Ascetics* (Yonkers, NY: St Vladimir's Seminary Press, 1985 [1960]), 8.

[2]Synaxarion for St Ephrem, see online at oca.org/saints/lives/2017/01/28/100328-venerable-ephraim-the-syrian.

[3]The title of the homily was drawn from a phrase found twice in Exodus (10.28; 34.12) and also in I Timothy (4.16).

[4]Quoted in Epiphanius, *Panarion* 76.4.2.

[5]See Philip Rousseau, *Basil of Caesarea* (Berkeley, CA: University of California, 1994), 112f.

[6]Acts 2.21, Acts 4.12.

[7]See Fr Thomas Hopko, *The Names of Jesus: Discovering the Person of Christ through Scripture* (Chesterton, IN: Ancient Faith Publishing, 2015).

[8]We can experience this with pets, too, although we generally name them more whimsically than we do our children. I know of an owner with a large, highly aggressive dog that had been given the name Cujo as a puppy after the rabid St Bernard in a Stephen King horror novel. The moniker became a semi-prophetic, partly because it affected the way people treated the animal. Naming a cat "Princess," or for that matter, "Cruella Deville," will not only reflect your own attitudes toward her but will play a part in how she lives out her life.

[9]Meletios Webber, *Steps of Transformation: An Orthodox Priest Explores the Twelve Steps* (Ben Lomond, CA: Conciliar Press), 58.

[10]Rom 7.15–8.2.

[11]Sakharov, Archimandrite Sophrony, *Saint Silouan the Athonite* (Crestwood, NY: SVS Press, 1999 [1991]), 42, then see pp. 208ff.

[12]From his spiritual autobiography, *My Life in Christ*, Part 2.

[13]St Nikolai Velimirovic, Homily 27, in *Homilies: A Commentary on the Gospel Readings For Great Feast and Sundays Throughout The Year,* Volume 2 (Birmingham, UK: Lazarica Press, 1998), 277.

[14]See Mother Mary and Kallistos Ware, trans., *The Lenten Triodion* (Boston: Faber and Faber, 1978), 200. Alternate translation.

[15]Rom 15.13–14.

5
Self-Esteem, Self-Denial, Self-Love

He who has learned to know the dignity of his own soul is in a position to know the power and the mysteries of the Godhead, and thereby to be the more humbled.

Spiritual Homilies of St Macarius[1]

Do not neglect the gift you have.

1 Timothy 4.14

There remains more to say about the self in the context of exploring our sinner identity. Here we will focus especially on three concepts within Christian tradition that have mixed reputations: self-esteem, self-denial, and self-love. A surface reading of traditional monastic literature yields the impression that our spiritual forebears took a dim view of self-love, praised self-denial, and shunned self-esteem like poison. Such a picture agrees with an image of Christianity—especially in its ascetical dimension—as a religion of guilt and self-loathing. And, in some contexts, it can be.

But the context for us is quite different and our task here is to take a closer look at each of these concepts. Our interest in how to properly regard ourselves as sinners is necessarily bound up in how to properly esteem and treat ourselves. The conclusions from the last chapter—that the self is good and cherished, but also broken and confused—will have a direct bearing on how we regard and treat that self.

Our modern society conveys mixed messages about how to treat the self, running from uncritical self-acceptance and self-indulgence, to setting unmeetable criteria for beauty and fitness. There is something good and true in the repeated calls to improve how we regard ourselves. "Low self-esteem," if understood in terms of self-loathing or insecurity rather than healthy humility, is a paralyzing thing, keeping us from achieving great things. It is also a destructive force. A person who hates himself will nearly always take that hatred out on other people. People with poor self-worth make the rest of the world suffer for it. Think of the mother who beats her children because what they do reminds her of all the things she hates about herself (especially if she was beaten by her own parents). Think of the blogger who pens endless hateful screeds against homosexuals, largely because he despises his own unacknowledged sexual struggles. Self-hatred rarely fails to be acted out on others. As the saying goes, "The devil rejoices twice," first at the sin, and then the havoc wreaked through ill-placed shame and self-loathing.

And then of course there is the damage to one-self. On the milder level, consider the person who is unaware of what she is truly capable of achieving, and is held back all his or her life by low self-esteem. Then there are all the other ways that people compensate for the wrong kind of self-abnegation, such as over-eating, compulsive shopping, or obsessive gambling. Consider too how many people in self-denigrating professions like pornography got to where they are precisely because they think of themselves as worthless, useless beings. They were taught to hate themselves, and these ways of life are the inevitable result of their own inner mantra, that becomes something like a self-fulfilling prophecy: I am garbage.

So the messages we hear, exhorting us to build up our self-esteem, are correct, but they go astray when they tell us to do so through an unbridled self-pampering, especially through unchecked consumerism. There must be different kinds of self-esteem, and it will be fruitful to see how the ascetical writers expound the concept further below.

Self-Acceptance

The media and the arts are also on target when they preach "self-acceptance," but only when by that term they mean the acceptance of one's genuine condition, giving thanks for its gifts and taking responsibility for correcting its flaws. But on the surface, society rarely conveys that message. It is more often telling us to "accept ourselves exactly as we are." What does that mean? Accept myself as being a short person? OK. Accept myself as slightly weird, different, quirky? Fine! Accept myself as shy and introverted? Accept myself as extroverted? Absolutely.

But what else is a person supposed to accept about himself "exactly as he is"? Accept his predilection for violent sex acts? Accept herself unconditionally as someone who lives to undermine others and destroy their relationships? Accept his manic obsession with his appearance? No. We do not accept such things about ourselves, as if they are good, requiring no change. We *name* them as sinful passions, as tendencies that we must transcend, by identifying them, surrendering them to God, and submitting to his will, and thus becoming *sober* and *whole*. So we have to discern this concept of self-acceptance thoughtfully as well.

Metropolitan Anthony of Sourozh said, in one of his informal talks to his parish, "Accept yourself, as a stone given to a sculptor. Accept how you are and that you need work to reveal the statue, i.e. what you truly can be."[2] In other words, reconcile yourself to being you, a beautiful creature but a work in progress. Accept also that you must give yourself over to God's sculpting. Because there are elements that need refining and others that need excision to reveal the genuine you.

Self-Esteem

Now, let's bring this back to self-esteem. Earlier I asserted that maintaining a healthy sense of your own worth is important. Does this contradict the *Philokalia* and other ascetical literature? They tell us repeatedly and emphatically to flee from it as you would run from a herd of demons. A couple of examples will suffice. The fourth-century ascetic Evagrios the Solitary observes, "In the whole range of evil thoughts, none is richer in resources than self-esteem; for it is to be found almost everywhere, and like some cunning traitor in a city it opens the gates to all the demons."[3] Likewise, the fifth-century St Mark the Ascetic says, "All vice is caused by self-esteem and sensual pleasure; you cannot overcome passions without hating them."[4] Earlier I noted the modern view that a poor sense of self-worth is at the root of so much human suffering: is there a complete conflict of opinion here?

One way to resolve the apparent contradiction is to plumb the actual meaning of the word used in the ascetical literature. The word in the original Greek that is nearly always translated into English as "self-esteem" is "*kenodoxia*." If we think etymologically, "*keno-doxia*" is literally idle or empty (*keno*) glorification (*doxa*), which is more precisely rendered as "vainglory."[5] The Greek lexicons translate *kenodoxia* as the "desire for and delight in praise and reputation." So, what we are to flee is not the proper esteem of the self, but vanity and its companions pride, inordinate self-love, self-obsession and the love of praise. In other words, what we are to shed is *self-esteem taken in all the wrong directions*. Vainglory is indeed a deadly significant sin that the ascetical writers are right to warn us against. Vainglory and conceit are self-esteem gone awry.

Once when I led a retreat on these subjects, I had just finished this talk about "self-esteem" in the monastic writings. Afterwards, after we all sat in silence for a few minutes, the woman next to me sighed and said, "I sure wish someone had told me that it was vainglory we were supposed to flee." One wonders how much unnecessary self-suppression has been caused by this odd decision to translate *kenodoxia*—which so obviously means "vainglory," as "self-esteem." Because just as there is vanity to flee, there is self-worth to cultivate. Let's say more on that.

Self-Care[6]

In all this, and despite all the confusing language, there is a consistent picture given us by our Fathers and Mothers in God. They were, after all, not only spiritual giants but also eminently practical. They knew both the beauty of the human person and the tendency towards distorting and sullying that beauty. They knew that our hearts must be thoughtfully cultivated, like plants. Different plants need different kind of care. The fourth-century Desert Mother Syncletica ranked thoughtful gardeners alongside doctors as good examples:

When [gardeners] see that a plant is of small stature and sickly, they water it profusely and care for it greatly, so that it will grow and be strong; while, when they see in a plant the premature development of sprouts, they immediately trim the useless sprouts, so that the plant does not quickly wither. Likewise, physicians give rich nourishment to some patients, prescribing that they walk, while to others they give a strict diet and require them to remain at rest.[7]

How we care for ourselves will differ from person to person. Sometimes, and for some people, that care will be exercised in nourishment, at other times in fasting.

At the Litany of Supplication prayed in the Orthodox Church we ask God for "all things good and profitable to our souls and bodies." A healthy self-love will lead us to do what is truly best for ourselves, soul and body, such that to care properly for them is the work of heaven. As St Dorotheos of Gaza writes: "The one who harms his own soul is . . . helping the devil. The one who seeks to profit his soul is cooperating with the angels."[8]

Our "inmost self," as St Paul put it, is beautifully formed in God's image, a thing of dignity and glory. It is to be tended and loved, holistically. In a homily attributed to the fourth-century Macarius of Egypt we read,

> Know your nobility and your dignity, how honorable you are, the brother of Christ, the friend of the King, the bride of the heavenly bridegroom. The one who has learned to know the dignity of his own soul is in a position to know the power and the mysteries of the Godhead, and thereby to be the more humbled.[9]

"Soul" here denotes the totality of the human being, whom—unlike even the angels—God created in his own image. The glory of the human being consists of body and soul. In other words, all of you. But notice that this awareness of our own nobility and dignity goes hand-in-hand with humility before God. They must exist in balance with each other.

The cultivation of a right self-esteem, self-care, and self-love is worth thoughtful reflection. Because the wrong kinds—vainglory, an exaggerated need for others' approval and affirmation—are pernicious. They tempt us to undermine other people, aggrandize ourselves, and generally forget God. But since we must care for ourselves, think about ourselves, reflect on ourselves, we have to find appropriate ways to do so. We do this both in general (as human beings in God's cherished image) and in particular (as specific persons each bestowed with unique vocations by God for the world). This is part of a healthy and genuine self-reflection. The trick is to steer clear of vanity. That means, for one, when you do self-reflect, keep it light. A good sense of humor about yourself helps immensely in this regard. Don't overdramatize either your sins or your virtues. Frankly, chances are good that neither are spectacular.

So we have to discern what suitable self-care is. It will certainly involve making sure you get the proper medical care, eat nutritiously, exercise, get enough sleep. (Seriously, do what it takes to address your lack of sleep. See a specialist if you need to.) Find the right balance of work and leisure. Read a good book. Watch a good movie. But self-care also involves a thoughtful denial of excesses. That means fasting in due season, working with purpose, and strictly limiting our pleasures and passions. Keep in mind that prayer is also self-care, as are silence, proper asceticism, confession of sins, humility, and repentance.

So we have come full circle. Because self-condemnation ("I am the worst of sinners") and the flight from vainglory and self-obsession are unrelated to "having a poor self-image," being insecure, or having obsessive guilt feelings. Proper self-condemnation and flight from vain obsessions actually free us from precisely these pathologies. They are instruments, paradoxically, of deep self-care. St Dorotheos of Gaza, whom we have been citing frequently, writes that lowliness of mind is the way to "all joy and all glory and all tranquility." He continues: "How much joy, how much peace of soul would a person not have wherever he went . . . if he was one who habitually accused himself . . . that person would have complete freedom from care."[10]

How do you know if you are conducting the "right kind" of self-condemnation? You'll know it by its fruit. If the result is not peace, freedom from care, joy, and absence from judgmentalism, then you are not using this tool as the saints intended. The saints say we can expect these effects if we use these tools correctly. Who among us would not like to experience them?

A Right Configuration

As the *New York Times* columnist David Brooks reminds us, St Augustine liked to speak of sin in terms of "disordered loves."[11] It is fitting to love oneself, one's family, God, as well as to enjoy things like food, sexual pleasure, and money. Sin comes when we prioritize these loves in the wrong order. We might likewise say that it can be appropriate to love ourselves and care for ourselves, as well as to condemn ourselves and discipline ourselves. We must, however, rank them in the proper configuration.

Amazingly, Augustine claims that balancing self-condemnation, self-love, and self-care is actually possible. Imagine yourself as someone who speaks without equivocation, and also understands how to keep silent. Someone with absolutely nothing to prove, to yourself or to anyone else, and doesn't require others' admiration. Someone who has come clean with God in your transgressions and who is, in fact constantly coming clean with him. Transparent to God, you have broken the shackles of self-justification, constantly trying to rationalize your sins. You have attained the humility of accepting God's love and forgiveness. Your goal is not to impress or to blame, and certainly not to judge anyone. That's the freedom attained through humility and repentance. That's genuine self-esteem: it moves you outside of your vanity and frees you to love God and be loved by him, to love others and be loved by them, to nurture others and be nurtured by them, and to love and care for your true, innermost self.

———

Humility is effectively a genuine, proportionate sense of oneself before God and others. It also denotes wholeness, or whole-mindedness, because our goal not to further fragment ourselves ("here's my good self, here's my bad self") but to be whole persons. It is this whole person—and not some kind of pious created persona—who presents himself before God in prayer. It is this whole person—and not some façade—who relates with himself and with others.

So, yes: the whole person that I am is indeed a sinner. My innermost, God-given beauty only barely shines through, distorted as I am by my enslavement to passions, to my will, and my need for gratification. Only in giving myself over to God can I hope to attain my freedom. Only then will my inner self shine. Only then will I be fully alive to the Glory of God. Then, too, I will know this "self" that I must care for diligently, with love and appropriate discipline.

May I learn to discern proper and true self-care, self-esteem, and true self-condemnation, that I may be free and whole, a loving consolation to others, and an active, breathing, fully-alive image of Christ.

Notes

[1]St Macarius, *Spiritual Homilies* 27.1. Translation from *Fifty Spiritual Homilies of St Macarius the Egyptian*, trans. A. J. Mason (New York: SPCK, 1921), 200 (translation updated).

[2]As recorded by Mary Ford, who took notes during his talks with parishioners.

[3]*Philokalia* Vol. 1, p. 46.

[4]*Philokalia* Vol. 1, p. 117.

[5]In Philippians 2.3, the Greek κενοδοξία is translated in the King James Version as "vainglory," and by the Revised Standard Version as "conceit."

[6]The following paragraphs, and the citations from St Dorotheos, are informed by talks that Metropolitan Anthony of Sourozh would give to his gathered parishioners. I am grateful to Mary Ford, who shared her notes from these talks.

[7]*The Evergetinos*, Book I, Vol. I (Etna, CA: CTOS, 1991), 21.

[8]*Discourses and Sayings*, 136.

[9]*Spiritual Homilies* 27, in *Fifty Spiritual Homilies of St Macarius*, 200 (translation amended).

[10]*Discourses and Sayings,* 141.

[11]See his *The Road to Character* (New York: Random House, 2015), 186–212.

6

The Sweetness of Compunction

May those who sow in tears reap with shouts of joy!

Psalm 126.5

Blessed are those who mourn, for they will be comforted.

Matthew 5.4

I t is time to take a deeper look at some of the benefits of coming clean with ourselves, each other, and God. As you might guess, we'll be rescuing yet another set of concepts from some of their negative connotations. "Regret" will be one, as well as "shame" and "guilt."

Each of these words has a justifiably bad reputation, because each so easily leads to destructive thoughts and behaviors. In the pages that follow, we'll be looking at regret (or compunction), beginning with a reflection on guilt and shame and the various ways to distinguish them. Because naming these phenomena and acting on them appropriately is a vital component of a life lived in freedom, grace, and clarity. And if the ancient Church writers are to be believed, traveling this path of sober self-scrutiny and reflection, mournful as it can be, also yields a profound sweetness.

Guilt and Shame

The media often stereotypes religious people as suffering from perpetual guilt complexes. In comic or dramatic portrayals guilt is usually presented as a burden to be shed, but sometimes as an appropriate emotion after wrongdoing. Let's reflect for a moment on guilt as well as shame, with which it is frequently associated.

First, they are states of being. "Guilt" means "culpability." A person who has committed a crime is guilty of that crime. I can be objectively guilty of an action, whatever the mitigating circumstances might be and however I might feel about it. I either did it or I didn't. Likewise, "shame" means "dishonor" or "humiliation." A person can "bring shame" to his or her family through behaving dishonorably.

What concern us here, in our reflection on the "sinner identity," are *feelings* of guilt and shame. (My observations below are superficial: there is much more to be said on this intricate subject, but I hope that even this level of reflection can be of use.) Guilt and shame may be experienced by an individual or a collective, such as a family, a society, a nation. They may act as a salutary warning-light; they may infect like a disease. But before we evaluate their merits and drawbacks, let's spend a few minutes looking at how guilt and shame are related, but distinguishable from each other in at least two ways.

Doing vs. Being

Some—including many psychologists—analyze guilt as a feeling about something that I have done, while shame is a feeling about something that I am. ("I *did* something bad," vs. "I *am* bad").

Within this distinction, guilt concerns things that are within your control to change or redirect. You can therefore acknowledge it, confess it, and take responsibility for it. You may be able to make reparations. And you can *repent* of it, working to reorient yourself in order not to repeat the problem behavior. It's therefore possible to be rid of the deed, so that the feelings around it no longer need to haunt you.

Shame, on the other hand, being about what you *are,* is outside your control. You can be ashamed of your height, your skin color, your social class. There's little or nothing to be done about these, so that feelings of shame are pointless and always to be avoided. The only way shame can be useful is if it is converted into guilt, in other words, into something that can indeed be changed, dealt with, and expunged.

This way of distinguishing the two is helpful in that it encourages us to identify what we can act on and what we can't. It directs us away from downward spirals of shame and toward reparative actions to free us from the weight of guilt. This is important and helpful.

But there is something in this distinction that rings false. For one, people don't only feel shame for things they are, for things that they cannot help. People can be ashamed also for things they have *done.* If I do something wrong (cheat on my spouse, say), I feel not only guilty, but ashamed of myself. In addition, I disagree that shame plays no useful role unless it is "converted" to guilt over something you can change. Shame can be both apt and healthy. Imagine someone who wantonly and repeatedly lies, steals, bullies people, or sleeps around. People will justly ask such a person: "Have you no shame?" Because in the face of some kinds of bad behavior, "You should be ashamed of yourself!"

The *Philokalia* talks about "shame" mostly as a descriptive of sins—the "shameful misdeeds" we should avoid. The implication there is always that we ought to feel ashamed for such wrongs, such that "feeling no shame" is seen as a problem. "Alas, alas, for I do not feel shame before my Creator and Master!"[1] At points, though, the feeling of shame is shown to be a possible aid to acquiring humility.[2]

Individual vs. Social

Another way to construe the distinction can be found in anthropological studies: guilt is an *individual* reaction ("I transgressed a law or commandment and I feel bad about what I did"), while shame is a *social* one ("I am embarrassed before others, and/or God, for what I did or who I am"). Guilt comes when *you* know you've done something wrong; you feel shame when *others* know it. It arises when you consider how they see you or your actions or have been affected by them. Guilt has to do with transgressing morality, shame with how others experience your actions.

This distinction also sounds realistic. However, separating out individual from social transgressions has an inherent flaw: nothing is a totally "individual act." Regardless of what other human beings have discerned about my misbehavior, inside myself I am fully aware that God knows about it. Furthermore, the whole universe is affected by it—such is our integral connection to all things. Which means that I might feel not only guilty but also ashamed for what I have done, even if I haven't gone public. In a spiritually interconnected world, nothing I do, say, or even think, stops with me.

When the Prophet Hosea wrote about the people's lack of faithfulness and kindness, their swearing, lying, killing, stealing, and adultery, he linked it directly with the demise of the soil and the animals:

> Therefore the land mourns,
> and all who dwell in it languish,
> and also the beasts of the field,
> and the birds of the air;
> and even the fish of the sea are taken away.[3]

On the spiritual level, the victimless crime is a nonreality. The whole world suffers from what I think and do.

Practical Lessons

Defining guilt in opposition to shame allows us to distinguish what we can control from what we cannot, and the realm of morality from that of self-regard. That is good. But distinctions between guilt and shame are not tidy, for in fact the two are often thoroughly interwoven. No matter how we define them they exist side-by-side. Let's say I consciously cheated on my taxes, so that I would pay less money to the government and keep more for myself. Provided I haven't been completely successful at justifying myself ("Taxes are too high anyway!" "I deserve this!" "It's not for me but for my family!") I may feel guilty, because I've done something objectively wrong. I may also feel ashamed, especially if I consider how my children would react if they knew. That combination pertains, in one configuration or another, to virtually any misdeed. It is often the shame of the guilty person that will lead him or her to change, to seek forgiveness, to surrender to God.

However we define shame and guilt, they come down to a mixture of feelings of regret, embarrassment, humiliation. Here are some steps toward taking a spiritually useful approach to them:

> 1. Identify what you are actually feeling

   2. Acknowledge it to yourself and to someone
      else
   3. *If it may be acted on, do so.*
   As soon as possible, let it go and move on.

St John Chrysostom reminds us that, just as shame follows a sin, so courage follows repentance.[4] That is a movement in the right direction.

Be patient. Every stage of this process can pose challenges. Although they may take only seconds or hours, on other occasions they may demand months or years. It also helps to know that along the way, feelings of shame or guilt may be entirely appropriate. They also might be instrumental. They can play a crucial role in the positive reorientation of our self-understanding and our relationship with God and the world.

These otherwise negative feeling can also help us participate in Christ, who—amazingly—*became* shame. That is how the Church speaks about Jesus and his death on the cross, which in historical context was one of the most shameful deaths to undergo.[5]

Since we're talking about practical lessons, let's dwell a bit longer on shame, over things that we can and can't control. Think about what these might be for you: the size of your feet, which sex attracts you, the social status of your ancestors. Begin by naming these sources of shame, as well as the fact that they are not your fault and mostly beyond your ability to change. Then you need to decide how to cope with such feelings. But it's important to identify what is and is not in your power to change, so as not to waste your efforts.

This is important. There may be events or aspects of your life that, through no fault of your own, you have been led to feel guilty about, sometimes devastatingly. Imagine you are the engineer of a commuter train, and someone dies by leaping in front of your fast-moving cab. Or you are pregnant and suffer a miscarriage. Or you are a surgeon whose patient dies on the table despite a flawless procedure. Perhaps you discover that your father or grandfather participated in war crimes. Or you are a victim of physical, emotional, and/or sexual abuse who—as is tragically common—feels responsible for acts perpetrated against you. The naming and healing of these wounds may take years.

This kind of shame is common to people regardless of their belief system. Christians have the gift of a God who knows shame and suffering, in the person of the Divine Son Jesus Christ. Through no fault of his own, he underwent utter shame and suffering. This was an act of total solidarity with us who experience our own shame. It also shows that within those depths of darkness there is a victory of light.

In all of this, the stakes are high—both positively and negatively. Feelings of repressed guilt and shame, unnamed, unchecked, untreated, can lead to emotional and physical illness. When turned inward, unchecked shame leads to depression, and possibly towards suicidal tendencies; when turned outward, it can lead to toxic anger, and possibly towards the abuse of oneself and others. In fact, people can seek to offset their own shame by shaming *others*. In one very common example of this, a man can so despise the fact that he is sexually attracted to other men that he channels that hatred towards others, especially other people with same-sex attraction. Shame can furthermore lead to or exacerbate compulsive and addictive behaviors, notably the abuse of substances, food, sex, or money. All of these are deeply serious concerns, a matter—sometimes literally—of life and death. Guilt and shame can act like a poison.

And yet, guilt and shame play a vital part in our salvation. Just as the body generates a fever to combat illness and nerves send signals of pain upon trauma, so our feelings of guilt and shame can tell us that a wrong needs to be rectified, a breach needs to be healed.

In fact, these kinds of remorse are signs that your conscience is in good working order (an important step in an examination of the self is acknowledging that it may not be). One of the most significant symptoms of our fallen human nature is that your ability to discern right from wrong is compromised. The instrument isn't properly calibrated. Add to this that you, like many of us, may have become experts in jamming its mechanism. You do that by justifying the transgressive things you think, say, and do. Many of us put a great deal of effort into that. Sinning can make us feel extremely good for a while, and we really want to continue! So we cloud our conscience, ignore it, or assuage it.

But this never actually benefits us, even though it is a perennial human pastime. We do it individually and corporately. Recently, one of the world's largest automobile manufacturers, Volkswagen, was caught cheating.[6] They installed a mechanism in their cars that lowered the vehicle's harmful emissions only when it was undergoing a diagnostic test. Basically, they found a way around the car's "conscience." Such bald-faced cheating is shocking. But we do much the same when we suppress our own consciences to do what we know is wrong.

* * *

So guilt and shame are signs of a healthy conscience, and in this—ironically, perhaps—they may even testify to a healthy sense of self-worth. A feeling of shame can be telling us, "You were created for better than this. You *are* better than this. This bad behavior is beneath the beauty and dignity of your true self."

We are now ready to talk about something that can encompass guilt and shame, and go beyond them.

Compunction

In Chapter 1 ("Discovering Myself as 'Sinner' "), I spoke of the importance for our journey of finding ourselves in contexts of purity and holiness. Sometimes, being with a truly good person—someone in conscious pursuit of purity and closeness to God—can alert us to our sinfulness. They can make us feel uncomfortable because, without any intention of embarrassing us, they see through our façades. The degree to which we experience holiness, wherever we find it, will likely be the degree to which we experience compunction. Not necessarily as remorse for a particular deed, but for our brokenness. Contrition is the natural reaction to the gulf between what we are in our disordered lives and what we are in God's eyes. Ideally our experience of that gulf will produce a positive, life-giving compunction.

The eighth-century saint Hesychios said much the same about the awareness and cultivation of this inner goodness:

> If we preserve, as we should, that purity of heart, the watch and guard of the intellect . . . this will not only uproot all passions and evils from our hearts; it will also introduce joy, hopefulness, compunction, sorrow, tears, an understanding of ourselves and of our sins, mindfulness of death, true humility, unlimited love of God and man, and an intense and heartfelt longing for the divine.[7]

The virtues and pursuits he lists have the effect of routing sinful passions and evil. These gifts help to explain why—consistently throughout the ancient prayer texts—we see the saints effectively *asking God for remorse*. For example, "Take from me the heavy yoke of sin, and in your compassion, grant me tears of compunction."[8] Or, " "Give me understanding, O Lord, that I may weep bitterly over my deeds."[9] These tears of contrition will lead us to a life lived truly.

But such an attitude, like everything we have been discussing in this book, is rife with the possibility of neurosis. For one, compunction needs to be distinguished from clinical depression, which as a chemical imbalance in the brain must be diagnosed and treated by a healthcare practitioner through therapy and/or medication. Without a modern clinical understanding of depression, St Paul recognizes the difference between therapeutic shame and the neurotic kind. To the Corinthians, he writes that "godly grief produces a repentance that leads to salvation and brings no regret, but worldly grief produces death."[10] Here is the backstory: St Paul had sent this community an earlier, difficult letter that had evidently caused considerable upset. But he is pleased about this, not because he takes any enjoyment in causing grief, but because he sees that the people acted on it. Their remorse lead them to address their problems so that they grew into a better community. St Paul's message is that sorrow is to be expected in this world. The problem arises when grief is allowed to fester and to destroy. Therefore we should embrace a compunction that compels us to change our lives for the better.

Elsewhere too, remorse takes its place among many benefits. Hear a list of encouragements given us by the angels: "support, illumination, compunction, encouragement, patient endurance, joyfulness, and everything that saves and strengthens and renews our exhausted soul."[11] Contrition, the ascetics say, is to prayer as salt is to food, and as melody to the lute. Without it, the meal has no flavor, the notes no sweetness.[12] Compunction, then, gives our inner life and our prayer life substance. It insures that our words are heartfelt and grounded in reality.

Reality as Sweetness

You may well wonder what is sweet about feeling shame and regret. I've discussed the benefits of these states of mind when they lead us to re-order our minds and lives for the better (in a word: repentance). I have suggested that contrition, properly felt, lends a genuineness to our actions and our prayers. Effectively, *compunction is reality*. What does that mean? Consider the opposite. If our stance, before others, ourselves, and God, has no reference to our mistakes, failures, misdirected priorities—none whatsoever—we are simply not in concert with reality. We are in denial.

In interviews with politicians or high-profile corporate officers they are often asked to list mistakes they have made in their careers. It's a risky question to answer, because such leaders want to project competence, and in some cases, avoid prosecution! Rarely will they understand that realistic self-scrutiny is a vital component of competence. Because almost inevitably, the subject will dance around the question and avoid it. And the only "regrets" they typically list in these cases are the shortcomings of *others*. The effect of these utterances is, simply put, unreal to a shocking degree. But even apart from the trickiness of public confession of sins, many of us tend towards that kind of fault-masking.

Part of the sweetness of compunction stems from owning up to actual reality. Shortcoming, failure, and brokenness are inevitable in the living of this life. Denial and justification lead to lies and are always harmful to us. Acknowledgement leads to authenticity. Confronting that reality may hurt, but only for a while. The fourth-century Egyptian ascetic John the Dwarf considers that the easy burden is self-accusation, while the heavy one is self-justification. Although it sounds counterintuitive, recognizing sin may seem a burden, but it beats the imprisonment of constantly lying to ourselves. Commenting on that observation, Rowan Williams explains that the burden of self-justification amounts to the ego's perennial trench-digging, in a futile effort to defend itself. Self-accusation, puzzlingly, is the light burden. Why? Because "we know that the burden is already known and accepted by God's mercy. We do not have to create, sustain, and save ourselves; God has done, is doing and will do all."[13]

People versed in psychology will know well the perils of covering up our compunction or sadness. Especially following tragedy, trauma, abuse, a loved one's death, we are apt to supplant our regret and sadness with other things such as forced joy, anger, hatred, anxiety, and/or depression. The therapy for deep-set and unexpressed sadness will often include prolonged tears, the welling up of what had perhaps long been submerged. Often unspeakably painful, this sweet reality that will, God willing, result in healing and wholeness.

Penitential Prayer as Sweetness

The Lenten periods are reckoned by the Church as sweet. The Friday before Meatfare Sunday, we sing, "Let us begin the fast with joy!" and read aloud from the Old Testament:

"Thus says the Lord of hosts: The fast of the fourth month, and the fast of the fifth, and the fast of the seventh, and the fast of the tenth, shall be to the house of Judah seasons of joy and gladness, and cheerful feasts . . ." (Zech 8.19)

Why is it that the most penitential services of the Church are so often seen as the most beautiful, even joyful? People seek them out. The first days of Great Lent feature evening services where we sing the long penitential Canon of St Andrew of Crete, which opens:

> How shall I begin to mourn the deeds of my
>   wretched life?
> Come, my wretched soul,
> and confess your sins in the flesh to the
>   Creator of all.
> From this moment forsake your former
>   foolishness
> and offer to God tears of repentance.

The text enumerates all the sinners of the Old and New Testaments. If I follow the words, I find myself confessing that my sins are worse than theirs. The Canon also catalogues the virtuous ones of the Bible, and I find myself singing that I have failed to imitate their goodness. The musical tonalities are somber, and the lighting is low, sometimes limited to just the candles.

Who wants to come to such a maudlin service? Apparently, a lot of people do. The Canon services are among the most heavily populated of the year in the many parishes I have attended. Artists, bankers, academics, doctors, construction workers, teachers, and office administrators come. My teenage children would insist on attending: "My favorite!" (actual quote). All of these people, prostrating themselves willingly, devoid of pathos, as the prayers are chanted—it's a sight to behold.

That being said, these services do not appeal to everyone. First time visitors can be shocked at the depth and severity of their penitence. But for those who understand their context, they feel heavenly. Through social media I asked friends in the Church why they thought these services were so curiously attractive. Some of their answers touch on how they help us recognize the depth of divine love and forgiveness.

The bright sadness of these services reveals something about joy, about love that doesn't skim over faults but encompasses and heals them.

It's the "no matter what" quality of forgiveness and love. You don't really see the divine love until you look at how poorly you've done, and then see that you are *still* beloved and accepted.

Others wrote about the services' honesty and how they put sin into the context of redemption, mercy, forgiveness.

Another wrote about the communal dimension of these confessions:

> These services are beautiful because we drop our shields and open up our hearts, and we realize that we are not alone: others have made mistakes, felt sorrow and pain, and all need to heal.

Another suggested that they connect us with an emotion that can be elusive in the rest of our lives. And then this same person wrote:

> Somehow the distance from woundedness to joy is shorter than the distance from happiness to joy.

This observation still has me reflecting in wonder.

A recurrent theme of this Canon is the inner beauty of the human person: it is marred by sin, but capable of restoration. That is what we are asking for.

> Through love of pleasure
> has my form become deformed
> and the beauty of my inward being has been
>   ruined.

The woman searched her house for the lost
coin until she found it.
Now the beauty of my original image is lost,
Savior,
buried in passions.
Come and as she did, search to recover it.[14]

The repentant spirit of the Church maintains that that Christ comes to bring back the beauty that we have tarnished, and that we can participate in that restoration.

The Canon services are special, deliberately so. In them we see how the Church's liturgical cycle are a masterpiece of pastoral management. We don't delve so deeply into our compunction throughout the whole church year; if we did, we couldn't bear it. We have to maintain a balance. During the seasons of fasting, we focus on our responsibility for sin. But we must never lose sight of our goodness, created by God, restored in his Son, by his Holy Spirit. The Church's liturgy is designed to show us how to fast and how to feast, how to lament and how to rejoice. It opens our hearts to an increasing acceptance these realities. Because until we allow them in, they can barely touch us.

Bright Sadness

When I was writing my book on the Estonian composer Arvo Pärt, I examined a quality to his music that a vast number of his listeners have commented on. He interweaves sorrow and joy, loss and hope, suffering and consolation.[15] This balance—entirely true to the reality of human life—is reflected in the ethos of the Church.[16] The Church's emphasis on our corporate and personal sin holds before us that reality that we normally seek to forget. The Church likewise never ceases to hold before us the joy of the resurrection, and the miracle of divine love, mercy, and forgiveness. It also brings us to recollect the beauty of the universe, which itself is an epiphany of God and which offers God constant praise.

But, let's face it, repentance can be extremely painful to experience. Tears are not always laced with sweetness. Sometimes they express anguish, profound regret, bitterness. These can last, unconsolably, for years. There may be no simple remedy for a transgression we have either done or had done to us. We have to acknowledge that some of our pain will endure as long as we live. But our faith maintains that God knows it fully, that he has taken it up in himself, and that *he is love and mercy*.

Furthermore, after some kinds of trauma or tragedy, penitence may not be a healthy focus. We've already looked at the kinds of seemingly inevitable but misplaced guilt that people may feel over events that had no control over. Such cases are more apt to demand a period of healing, sometimes over a long time, before a person would profitably revert to the sinner language about himself or herself.

Keeping these caveats in mind, we find that the Church teaches there is consolation in our compunction, especially when it includes self-examination, identifying our sinfulness. Self-pity, blaming others, and self-justification play no part in that kind of repentance. In Step 7 ("On Mourning") of St John Climacus' *Ladder of Divine Ascent*, he notes that self-condemnation can be misapplied. He has read St Paul, and is aware of both good ("godly") grief and bad ("worldly") grief, that there is mourning, and there is "false mourning." But if we do it right, mourning is tinged with joy:

> When I consider the actual nature of compunction
> I am amazed at how that which is called mourning
> and grief should contain joy and gladness interwoven within it like honey in the comb. What then
> are we to learn from this? That such compunction

is a special sense a gift of the Lord. There is then in the soul no pleasureless pleasure, for God consoles those who are contrite in heart in a secret way.[17]

Climacus suggests that we are aiming for the right motivation. Compunction and mourning need to be driven less by sorrow than by love. May this mystery be revealed to us ever more, as we draw nearer to the loving God in the prayer life of the Church.

Notes

[1] Peter of Damaskos, in *Philokalia* Vol. 3, p. 112.

[2] See, for example, Diadochos of Photike, in *Philokalia* Vol. 1, p. 280.

[3] Hos 4.1–3.

[4] *On Repentance and Almsgiving,* Homily 8.

[5] See Gal 3.13—Christ redeemed us from the curse of the law, having become a curse for us—for it is written, "Cursed be every one who hangs on a tree."

[6] http://www.nytimes.com/2015/09/19/business/volkswagen-is-ordered-to-recall-nearly-500000-vehicles-over-emissions-software. html, accessed January 15, 2016.

[7] St Hesychios the Priest, *On Watchfulness and Holiness*, in *Philokalia* Vol. 1, p. 181.

[8] The Great Canon of St Andrew of Crete.

[9] The Canon of Repentance.

[10] 2 Cor 7.10.

[11]St John of Karpathos, *For the Encouragement of the Monks in India*, *Philokalia* Vol. 1, 315.

[12]Elias the Presbyter, *Philokalia* Vol. 3, 56; 46.

[13]Rowan Williams, *Silence and Honey Cakes,* 47.

[14]The Great Canon of St Andrew of Crete, a penitential work, devotes much of its second ode to reflection on the original beauty in which we were created, thus simultaneously lamenting our fall, and remarking that the glorious image is still there, and to be valued and recovered.

[15]Peter C. Bouteneff, *Arvo Pärt: Out of Silence* (Yonkers, NY: SVS Press, 2015).

[16]See also Fr Alexander Schmemann, *Great Lent: Journey to Pascha* (Yonkers, NY: SVS Press, 1974), 36 and elsewhere.

[17]St John Climacus, *The Ladder of Divine Ascent*, Step 7.49.

7
Mercy, Forgiveness, and Divine Judgment

I am the foremost of sinners; but I received mercy for this reason.

1 Timothy 1.15–16

God loves your enemies as much as he loves you.

Mother Gavrilia

A healthy approach to yourself as sinner depends upon knowing something of God's mercy. Without faith and trust in God—as merciful and loving beyond measure—our self-condemnation would be impossible to bear. It would be self-destructive. And there is no clearer portrait of God than the crucified Christ, who has voluntarily surrendered everything for us. The cross—the limitless self-giving, voluntary co-suffering that it represents, the extent of love and mercy that it conveys—reveals to us what it is to be God. Some theologians say that God is "cross-shaped."

"Yours it is to have mercy on us and to save us, O our God," we say in several Orthodox prayers. Forbearance is what God does, who he is, and we know this because he has shown us, again and again. *This* God, and none other, is the one before whom we acknowledge our sin, to whom we surrender the totality of our inner pollution. "Mercy" is the usual translation for the Greek *eleos* and the Hebrew *hesed*. Both *eleos* and *hesed* are also rightly rendered as "loving-kindness." Both also imply "grace," in the sense that this love is undeserved. It is pure and voluntary on the part of the bestower. The Greek *eleos* also calls to mind "oil" (in Greek *elaion*), which carries its own scriptural depth of meaning as an anointing of rulers,[1] something to make the face shine,[2] the oil of gladness.[3] Mercy, though, in the church context is primarily an unearned blessing from God.

It also means letting someone off the hook for a deserved penalty. Some years ago I was pulled over on the highway for speeding. I recall asking the policeman, "Would you have mercy on me?" His answer was brief and final: "No." (He proceeded to write me an extremely expensive ticket.) We beg the mercy of someone capable of condemning us to or releasing us from a penalty. We ask God's mercy in this sense as well. He is the judge. And it is a good thing that his justice does not mimic our own.

Divine Justice

Divine forgiveness bears little resemblance to our human sense of justice. Conceived humanly, justice consists of a fair trial and a reasonable punishment or reward. But if we are truly cognizant of the errors of our ways, we can only repeat the words of the psalm,

> If you, Lord, kept a record of sins,
> Lord, who could stand? But with you there is
>   forgiveness.

(Ps 130.3–4)

If God were "fair" or "just" according to human legal standards we would stand condemned. It's that simple. The ways we live for gratification, attach ourselves to possessions and pleasures, regard our colleagues and neighbors coldly and competitively, strew trash over the beauty of the world, and otherwise manifest our skewed priorities would find us condemned in an earthly court. But—thankfully—God's weighs justice differently.

> For my thoughts are not your thoughts,
> neither are your ways my ways, says the Lord.
> For as the heavens are higher than the earth,
> so are my ways higher than your ways
> and my thoughts than your thoughts.
>
> (Is 55.8–9)

Also,

> For as the heavens are high above the earth,
> so great is his steadfast love toward those who
>   fear him;
> as far as the east is from the west,
> so far does he remove our transgressions from
>   us.
>
> (Ps 103.11–12)

Heaven and earth, East and West—these describe a cross, of the greatest expanse imaginable.

The knowledge of this undeserved and unconditional forgiveness is the indispensable accompaniment to our compunction and our shame. It converts contrition into consolation and hope. As Pope Francis recently said, "Shame is a grace that prepares us for the embrace of the Father, who always forgives and always forgives everything."[4]

Identification and Confession

If naming ourselves as sinners rests in genuine self-understanding, before God, others, and ourselves, that means that recognition of that identity is a vital first step towards healing and mercy. The second step involves articulation. Openly acknowledging and articulating our wrongs to one another is a powerful medicine against the sickness of sin.

I may transgress against others—lie to them, hurt them physically or emotionally—and acknowledge it, but there is no guarantee that they will forgive me immediately—or ever. By contrast, we are told that mercy and forgiveness from God is instantaneous and guaranteed. The parable of the Prodigal Son depicts God as a father who runs with arms outstretched to embrace and kiss the son who intends to articulate his immorality. The father doesn't even allow his son to complete his confession—he has already ordered the celebratory feast (Lk 15.20–24).

You may prefer to bottle up your faults. It seems easier in the short term, after all. But the way to mercy and freedom comes through verbally owning up to them:

Happy are those whose transgression is
   forgiven,
    whose sin is covered.
Happy are those to whom the Lord imputes no
   iniquity,
    and in whose spirit there is no deceit.
While I kept silence, my body wasted away
   through my groaning all day long.
For day and night your hand was heavy upon
   me;
    my strength was dried up as by the heat of
    summer.
Then I acknowledged my sin to you,
   and I did not hide my iniquity;
I said, "I will confess my transgressions to the
   Lord,"
    and you forgave the guilt of my sin.
. . . Be glad in the Lord and rejoice, O
   righteous,
   and shout for joy, all you upright in heart.

                          (Ps 32)

Happiness relies on not deceiving yourself, but on acknowledging your errors and receiving forgiveness. Doing this with someone, usually a "confessor," does several things. It instills an accountability to another flesh-and-blood person—who also may be able to give some useful advice. It puts you into community with other sinners-being-forgiven, sufferers-being-healed, in the Church. And in all of this it takes you out of a very unhealthy isolation. No longer are you carrying a burden by yourself, you are giving it over to others, and ultimately to God.

And, again, God is merciful. Christ, our true judge and priest, is not "unable to sympathize with our weaknesses"; rather he "in every respect has been tempted as we are, yet without sin. *Let us then with confidence draw near to the throne of grace, that we may receive mercy and find grace to help in time of need.*"[5]

The State of Sinfulness

I opened this book with a description of three imaginary people with different approaches to the "sinner" identity. Let me describe a fourth, an actual historical figure, Peter of Luxembourg, from the 14th century. Throughout his youth, he was obsessed with identifying and cataloguing his transgressions. He would write them down in notebooks or on little scraps of paper. He would call for confession, twice a day and sometimes at night, too. Priests would try to ignore his pleas, but in vain. After his death (at the age of 18), they found a whole chest-full of these little scraps of paper with his sins.[6]

When I first read this story, my immediate reaction was that this kid really needed was to get a life. I don't wish to denigrate a Roman Catholic saint, but the accounts about him sound a bit unhealthy. He certainly lacks the post-confessional joy, that sense of relief that I've been touting. He seems to indulge in an obsessive-compulsive series of confessions. I wondered at his capacity for locating particular sins at every moment of his life—and then I had to ask whether doing so was really the point of Christian life.

You do need to come clean about particular faults and ill-directed tendencies. But specific sins do not tell the whole story. They may serve as indicators of patterns that deserve our attention. We may benefit from the insights of a spiritual director or an astute, trusted friend. For example, if I tend to feel bitter anger at people who disagree with me, I might harbor a kind of vanity, a self-esteem problem that I would do well to address. That tendency might also be thoroughly enmeshed with compulsions to overeating, lust, or other kinds of consumption and objectification. I need to be helped through that tangle of passions and attachments.

Another aspect of focusing on particular offenses is that they are but signs of an entire state of being. Whether or not I point to an exact quantity or gravity of specific faults I have committed, I will gradually come to understand myself as a sinner, in the sense of an overarching portraiture, my existential state. My *condition* of unworthiness brings me to my utter contingency upon God and his divine grace. The condition of "unworthiness" doesn't mean "I'm not worth saving." It means that I'm dependent on God's mercy, which I did not earn.

Imperfection and sin, as a total condition, are the doors to mercy. Orthodox Christians are not the only ones who recognize this. The 13th-century mystic poet Rumi writes, "The wound is the place where the light enters you." Eight hundred years later, Canadian songwriter Leonard Cohen would sing, "There is a crack in everything. That's how the light gets in." Trappist monk Thomas Merton wrote about the person who is "unafraid to admit everything that he sees to be wrong with himself, and yet recognizes that he may be the object of God's love precisely because of his shortcomings." Such a person, Merton continues, "can begin to be sincere. His sincerity is based on confidence, not in his own illusions about himself, but in the endless, unfailing mercy of God."[7]

Asking for God's Mercy

We have established at many points in this book that God is merciful by default. He forgives what we would consider unforgivable. He loves us more than we can comprehend. If this is the case, we might wonder: why do we need to ask for mercy?

It is the nature of a vending machine to dispense things. I put my coins in, and out comes the candy. I don't "humbly ask" the machine for its goods, nor am I grateful to it for dispensing them. The machine is just doing what it was made to do. God is obviously not a vending machine. But still, if God is the very definition of all-encompassing love and mercy, why not just rely on his forbearance to just "happen" to us?

At the human level, it's easier to understand the importance of asking forgiveness of each other. If I feel hurt by something my wife has said or done, I am inclined to forgive her, out of a combination of love, understanding, and even self-preservation. It isn't always easy. But if she comes to me and asks my forgiveness, my feelings are transformed. Almost immediately, I'm twice as ready to patch things up with a heartfelt embrace.

But this is not how God operates. God does not change his orientation towards us on the basis of how persistently we beg. Some Bible stories make it seem otherwise, but those narratives describe how we human beings experience God's love, mercy, and judgment. They show what seem to be give-and-take or tug-of-war exchanges between God and humans (especially in the Old Testament). If read without discernment, these paint a misleading portrait of God's nature, as our human perspective is limited. God's disposition towards us, personally and corporately, is unchanging whether we repent or defy him.

So, why ask for mercy and forgiveness?

For one, asking is a healthy part of how we respond to the realization of our shortcomings. In this sense, it's conceivable to ask (or at least to want to ask) forgiveness of an infant whom I caused to cry, of a dog whose paw I accidentally trod on, even of a place that I have defiled. None of these know or care whether I've sought their absolution. I ask because *I* need to. But once I have made the request to my clueless victim, I would hope to act differently. Saying, "I am sorry" begins as a realization of my negative effect on the wider world, evolves as a kind of self-cleansing, and then ought to be part of a commitment to act better in the future. Saying it aloud helps my apology become simultaneously a sign and an instrument of transformation.

Likewise petitioning aloud the merciful God, "Forgive me," or "Have mercy on me," is in part a pledge to do better. Before that, it acts as an acknowledgment, an inner reminder, of my total dependence on him. I am contingent on God for my very being. I seek that mercy in recollection of God's glory and greatness, his identity as creator and redeemer of the world, and also his role as judge of the world.

Moreover, my plea for forgiveness is a sign that I am willing to receive forgiveness. God doesn't force anything on us, not even his mercy or salvation. The 20th-century Russian-French theologian Vladimir Lossky wrote that God willingly becomes powerless in front of human freedom, "a beggar of love waiting at the soul's door without ever daring to force it."[8] Therefore I must become complicit with God's mercy and love. I can only do that if I am convinced that I need it.

God doesn't need us to ask for mercy in order to be merciful. He doesn't need us to ask for forgiveness, to forgive us. God, in his essence, doesn't need prayers of any kind. Our prayers and pleas, our exclamations of gratitude, both testify to and shape our disposition before him. They serve to cultivate and strengthen that stance, of contingency, gratitude, repentance, and joy. So much of prayer shapes us, softens our hearts, and allows us to wonder at the ways of God, the mercy of God, the justice of God, which—thank God—are not like ours.

God's Mercy and Mine

Telling his followers that they must love their enemies, Jesus says, "Be perfect, therefore, as your heavenly father is perfect." Thus says Jesus in Matthew's Gospel (5.48). In Luke's Gospel, the saying is just a bit different: "Be merciful, just as your Father is merciful" (6.36). One wonders, was Jesus making two different statements? Did Matthew and Luke hear the same thing differently, "Be perfect" versus "Be merciful"? Or perhaps we can glean that perfection is somehow related to mercy. Evidently, Jesus wants us to imitate God in his perfection and in his mercy.

These are two key places where Jesus tells us to pattern our behavior on God's. In another, he recites in the Lord's Prayer, "Forgive us our trespasses"—in other words have mercy on us in the face of our sins—"*as we* forgive those who trespass against us.*" He seems to be saying that we shouldn't ask God to absolve us if we don't absolve others. It's as if we are saying, "To the extent I forgive others, forgive me." Or at the very least we pray this as our commitment to try to forgive as God does, to have mercy as God does.

If nothing else, relating our forbearance to God's reminds us that the more we are aware of our own sin and our dependence upon God's endless grace, the more we will be compassionate towards others. This kind of reciprocity ought to come naturally, but often falls short. In Matthew's Gospel (18.23–35) Jesus tells a cautionary tale of a servant who was forgiven a huge debt by his master. When that servant was ruthless to his fellows who owed him money, the master imprisoned him. We might say that the inability to forgive is itself a prison.

At the end of St John's Gospel, Jesus breathes on the disciples, saying, "If you forgive the sins of any, they are forgiven; if you retain the sins of any, they are retained" (Jn 20.23). These words herald the disciples' future ministries. But we can also apply them universally. When we "retain" our own sins or those of other people, everyone is affected, on earth as in heaven.

But, hard as it might be, when we forgive, "let go and let God," everyone is freed.

There has been a debate on-and-off throughout the history of the Christian Church as to whether God might in fact save everyone. This is known as "the doctrine of universal salvation," often known by the Greek word *apokatastasis,* which means "restoration." From antiquity until today, many people reasoned that, since God is merciful and loving—essentially and by definition—and since evil is really only a misuse of good, it would follow that in the end, everyone will be saved, admitted into heaven. The Orthodox have been cautious of teaching universal salvation for a variety of reasons. For example, God doesn't interfere with human freedom, including the freedom to fall—but several of the Church's cherished voices have expressed at least the hope for the salvation of everything and everyone. Among those voices was St Silouan the Athonite. He once found himself in conversation with a hermit who took a certain relish in contemplating how God would send atheists to hell, because "it was their own fault." Silouan, alarmed and sorrowful, replied, "Love could not bear that . . ." Did he mean God's love, or ours? We don't know for sure, but he completed his sentence with ". . . we must pray for all."

Whether God saves everyone or not, we can hope that he does. But more than that, God's universal salvation or "*apokatastasis*" may in some way be predicated on my personal "*apokatastasis*," my internal complicity with universal divine mercy. As Jesus says, "whatever you bind on earth shall be bound in heaven, and whatever you loose on earth shall be loosed in heaven" (Mt 18.18). We might therefore consider adopting a practice of mercy, of "loosing," opening our hearts to God's salvation of everyone. Every single person we encounter—in a meaningful way, positively or negatively, or just in passing on the street, whether they are openly transgressing or seem deplorable or just annoying—is someone who should elicit our internal disposition of release. The next time you see someone you are inclined to judge, roll your eyes at, or condemn, imagine God calling you by name to say. "I love this person, and I want to save her. Is that OK with you?" Your answer should be, simply *must* be, "Yes, Lord! Don't let me hold you back!" That goes for everyone and anyone. The sea of people crowded ahead of you in the supermarket check-out lane. The kid with the ridiculous tattoo. That over-affectionate couple. Someone yelling at you because of your color or sex. The politician whose views you abhor. Every one of them:

"Yes." "Yes." "Yes! Save and love them, O Lord! And I will rejoice."

Technically speaking, God doesn't need our agreement to save someone, or for that matter to do anything he pleases. But he awaits our assent nonetheless. He won't even save *me* without my saying "yes" to it. So let me say "yes" to God's saving everyone and anyone. And then let me say "yes" to God's saving even myself.

This kind of "applied mercy" on other people, including the annoying or even morally reprehensible ones, should ideally entail that I also be willing to act an instrument in their salvation. In addition to assenting to their salvation, I should engage with them, listen to them, serve them. We will fall short of this ideal. But let's at least start with the "Yes." For everyone. The "personal *apokatastasis*" liberates others, and us too. It saves us the trouble—really the utter nuisance—of being judgmental. It is part of surrendering to God. As St Paul writes, "Let all bitterness, wrath, anger, clamor, and evil speaking be put away from you, with all malice. And be kind to one another, tenderhearted, forgiving one another, even as God in Christ forgave you" (Eph 4.31–32). Or as Jesus said, "Be merciful as your heavenly Father is merciful."

Summary

Throughout this book we have been looking at the healing power as well the potential problems of the sinner dynamic. Here is a brief summary to reflect on.

We've been describing the healthy appropriation of "sinner" language and identity as a journey, and any of a number of pitfalls can crop up along the way. In fact, it's best to expect that they will so you won't be taken by surprise when it happens. These are some of the toxic tendencies to beware of when taking on a sinner identity.

- Reactivating old abuse/victim language about yourself.
- Exacerbating a genuine clinical depression.
- Descending into shame-spirals over things you can't control.
- Obsessing over past sins that have already been forgiven.
- Thinking that you *are* your sin, your shame, your guilt.
- Becoming maudlin or self-pitying.
- Trying to "out-unworthy" other people.
- Allowing it to prevent you from living a fully realized life.

Be patient with yourself. Don't forget to pray.

As for the healing tendencies of the penitential mindset, St Paul identified "the fruits of the Spirit," as "love, joy, peace, patience, kindness, goodness, faithfulness, gentleness, self-control" (Gal 5.22). Here's what you might discover in yourself as symptoms or consequences of understanding yourself properly as a sinner:

- Living in truth.
- A right stance before God and your fellow humans.
- Freedom from enslavement to self-justification.
- Freedom from care about what others think of you.
- Freedom from taking offense.
- Freedom from judging others.
- Love and mercy for others.
- Love for your true, innermost self.
- Taking responsibility for wrongdoing.
- Addressing your attachments, compulsions, and passions.
- Experiencing forgiveness and love.
- Knowing the sweetness of unearned love.
- Inner peace.

- An appreciation of beauty and goodness in the world.
- The discernment of evil in the world.
- Closeness to Christ.
- Greater knowledge of Christ, who saves the world, overcomes evil, and forgives sin.

Epilogue

Coming to understand yourself as a sinner heals you because it lets you acknowledge a truth about yourself. It bolsters your consciousness of goodness, beauty, and God. It breaks the logjams that separate you from your true self, from your fellow humans, from God, and from the created world. It is the beginning of your inner acceptance of God's all-encompassing and unconditional love. It sets you free.

The classical icon of Christ's descent into Hades is evocative of much of this. The "Easter icon," as it's often called, shows him standing on the gates of hell which he broke down. Around the shattered doors are dozens of broken locks. Surrounded by others whom he saves, he pulls Adam and Eve (representing all of fallen humanity) out of the imprisonment of Hades (representing death).

When Christ, the God-man, *becomes* sin and *enters* death, they cease to be what they were. They are no longer final, they no longer reign over us. Their power is gone. Jesus's death completes God's entry into the full extent of our vulnerability, our susceptibility, our imprisonment. There's nowhere lower he could go, no further depth he could have penetrated. The greatest abyss, the deepest darkness is now filled with the true Light. Darkness, captivity, and sin have lost any power they might have had over us. All is light.

All we have to do is prefer the light. That means letting it engulf us, illumine us, expose us for everything we've done and for what we are. It means surrendering, as sinners, to God's mercy and love.

Notes

[1]Ex 29.7.

[2]Ps 104.15.

[3]Ps 41.7; Heb 1.9.

[4]Public address at St Peter's Square, August 2, 2015. See http://www.catholicnews.com/services/englishnews/2015/dont-be-afraid-or-ashamed-to-go-to-confession-pope-says.cfm, accessed January 15, 2016.

[5]Heb 4.15–16, italics added.

[6]This description of the life of Peter of Luxembourg is from Johan Huizinga, *The Waning of the Middle Ages* (Mineola, NY: Dover, 1999 [1924]), 168.

[7]*No Man is an Island* (New York: Harcourt, 1955).

[8]Lossky, *Orthodox Theology: An Introduction* (Crestwood, NY: SVS Press, 1978), 73.

THEOLOGICAL APPENDICES

This book has featured many observations about human beings, their beauty and their fallenness. What are my source data on these subjects? I am drawing on my experience as a human being, as a sinner, and as a student and professor of theology committed to the life and teaching of the Orthodox Church. The following two appendices set out my understanding of the Church's basic teachings about these two subjects, with the hope of providing a deeper foundation to what we've been talking about in the preceding pages.

1

The Bible on Human Nature: Is It Human to Sin?

What are human beings that you are mindful
*   of them,*
mortals that you care for them?

Psalm 8.4

What it means to call myself "a sinner" invites some basic questions about identity: "Who am I?" and "Am I good or bad?" These are grounded in another fundamental question: "*What* am I?" To this you could answer, "I am a human being," but you know what the next question is: "What is a human being?"

How do you evaluate a specific guitar, or a table, or a horse, or a car? How do you decide whether it is good or bad, lacking or complete? You do so on the basis of what guitars, tables, or horses are collectively, on how they must function, and how they ought to perform. Guitars are supposed to sound resonant and be readily playable. Tables ought to be level and stable. We assess any particular guitar or table against those kinds of criteria. It follows that the questions I ask about myself—my identity, my evaluation of myself, and God's evaluation of me—are characterized by the general questions about humans collectively. Questions about the particular (me) need to be informed about the general (humanity). Plus they need to be informed by function: what is the purpose of human beings?

Genesis 1–3:
The Nature of Good (But Fallen) Humanity

The first three chapters of Genesis exist largely in order to answer exactly these basic questions about what it means to be human and how we relate to God. Most everyone is familiar with their broad contours. The first chapter narrates the six days/events of God's bringing the world into existence. The next two chapters focus on the odyssey of the human person by recounting the story of the primordial couple Adam and Eve. Over many millennia these chapters have been interpreted in a variety of ways. They leave many questions unanswered about astronomical, geological, and biological origins. But Genesis was never intended to address those questions. The early Christian interpreters didn't consult it in order to learn about the physical history or layout of our solar system. But they did use it to glean key insights about how the human person relates to God and the rest of creation.[1]

Here are some of the relevant teachings that the early Christian authors consistently found the in Genesis 1, a chapter sometimes known as the "Hexaemeron" or six days:

- **God orders the world in a deliberate way.** Whatever the "days" signify (24-hour cycles? millennia? sets of events?), they reveal God working through a purposeful sequence of creative acts. We witness God forming the universe out of nothing and setting it in careful order.

- **The human being is the pinnacle of creation.** After all the "Let there be"s of the first five days, suddenly God takes stock within himself and says "Let *us* make man" (in Hebrew, "*adam*"). God creates the human person, male and female, in his own image, i.e., making us a unique reflection of himself within creation (Gen 1.26–27).

- **Creation—with humanity—is very good.**
  God evaluates creation as "good" at every stage.
  But once he creates humanity, he considers it to
  be *very* good (Gen 1.31).

Within creation, then, humanity is both good and
uniquely akin to divine nature. These points must inform
our inquiry about ourselves at every stage.

The next two chapters of Genesis focus on Adam
and Eve in Paradise. Here the early Christian interpreters glean further basic truths about humankind:

- **Humanity is a community, male and female.**
  The first time that God says "it is not good" is
  when he considers the man alone. The human
  person is communal, and sexed, by nature. In
  Genesis 5.2, during a summary of Genesis 1–3,
  we learn that it is only when there are male
  and female that God even calls us "human" (in
  Hebrew, *adam,* in Greek, *anthrōpos*).

- **Humanity is good, but fallen.** Created as
  God's reflection and animated with God's breath,
  human beings are given the promise of immortal-
  ity and perfection. But they do not realize their
  potential. They live in a state of child-like inno-

cence, naked and unashamed, and in that state they succumb to a foreign influence.

- **Humanity is supposed to become like God, but not magically.** Humans yield to the temptation of the forbidden fruit because the devil tells them it will make them like God (Gen 3.5). Of course, God *created* us to be like him, but we were not supposed to achieve that by eating a magic fruit. Instead, our "divinization" is meant to happen in more beautiful and enduring ways that involve conscious co-operation with God.

- **Humanity is fallen.** This is an important point for a book about sinning. Genesis shows us that we fell, that we are broken. Since the fall, we have never known any other mode of existence, which inevitably ends with our biological death.

- **Humanity is still good.** In spite of the fall, the fact remains that we were created good and are good. The fall does not result in our being totally depraved, stripped of all virtue or reason. Our fallenness, our errors, our shortcomings do not define what it means to be human. True humanness is sinless.

- **Humanity is an organic, interconnected whole.** As the Genesis story continues, we see how people beget other people, and sin begets sin. One leads to another. The immorality of one person affects his fellows. No person's holiness or sin exists in isolation from others. We are so interconnected with one another and intertwined with the rest of creation that our sin even affects the natural world (Is 24.5; Hos 4.2–3; Rom 8.19–23).

So when humanity fell from grace, our goodness became complicated. Our perception of reality got clouded. Our moral compass and our motivations were compromised. And we live under the specter of death.

Keep in mind that, although the book of Genesis was written in a Jewish context, the Christian Church cannot read it without interpreting it in terms of Jesus Christ. That's because Christ is the one by whom the world was made (Jn 1.3). Christ is the creator; he pervades the universe; he is its principle of coherence. When the compiler of Genesis narrates the creation of light, of water, of humans, Christian thinkers are reminded that Christ is the true Light and the living Water. They also understand that Christ is the New Adam (Rom 5.14). Christ, our full and final redemption, is the Logos, the "logic" and coherence of everything that is shown in Genesis 1–3, and beyond.

> For in [Christ] all things were created, in heaven and on earth, visible and invisible, whether thrones or dominions or principalities or authorities—all things were created through him and for him. He is before all things, and in him all things hold together. (Col 1.16–17)

Christ, the New Adam, is the redemption of the human person. He is perfection. The Old Adam is *not* perfection: having squandered his potential, he represents human brokenness. When we look to Adam and Eve we see the story of the struggle to obtain goodness—sometimes finding it and sometimes not. The entire biblical story shows God calling us, God redeeming us. Sometimes we act on that redemption, more often we do not.

God allows our downfall in order to help us become discerning creatures. That gives us the chance to choose freely, informed by real experience. God respects us too much to create us as automatically good: genuine love cannot be pre-programmed. By design, we are in a state of emerging. We are made in God's image—the fall doesn't take that away—but we must actively participate in the process of becoming truly like him, being "perfect as our heavenly father is perfect" (see Mt 5.48). God, in his Christ and by his cross, sets us on the way. Our challenge is to accept the journey.

Human creation required only one unilateral initiative: God's. But our redemption requires bilateral measures: God's and ours. God doesn't force us to be like him. God creates by his own will but he voluntarily submits himself to our cooperation. He will not violate that principle of freedom, love, and respect.

To sum up what it is to be human:

- Good but fallen

- Fallen but redeemed

- Redeemed but with responsibility in community and in Christ

Genesis shows that humanity and human experience cannot be described with a single unqualified adjective. Humanity is complex and finite. God, on the other hand, is simple and infinite, and his approach to us can be described in just one word: Love.

Further Reflections

1. The Psalms: The Experience of Being a Good-but-Fallen Person

If the Genesis creation accounts offer insights into our origins, our transgression, and God's redemption, the Psalms immerse us into how we experience these realities in this world. The Psalms are a catalogue of human frustration, hope, despair, faith, trust, anger, love. Every one of these human dispositions is given its due, along with its proper orientation.

Psalm 8 gives a perfect introduction as to who and what we truly are. It opens in the praise of the wondrous God:

> O Lord, our Lord,
> how majestic is thy name in all the earth!
> Thou whose glory above the heavens is
> chanted by the mouth of babes and infants
>
> . . .

In the face of that glory, and the glory of the rest of creation, human beings seem so small:

> When I look at thy heavens, the work of thy
> fingers,

> the moon and the stars which thou hast
>   established;
> what is man that thou art mindful of him,
> and the son of man that thou dost care for
>   him?

And yet the creator has made us great, like he himself is:

> Yet thou hast made him little less than God,
> and dost crown him with glory and honor.

The only adequate response is to return to the praise and awe of God:

> O Lord, our Lord,
> how majestic is thy name in all the earth!

But our greatness stands in stark contrast to the ways in which we sin. We make war; we act wickedly. The rich oppress the poor. Immorality appears throughout the Psalms, in terms that are all the more stark and emotional given humanity's rootedness in virtue and the glory with which we were crowned. Our hope rests not in us, but in God. God made us majestic and remains our redeemer. It is God in whom we should put our faith, say the Psalms.

The Psalms describe a constant movement from lament to praise, despair to hope, frustration to faith, and we can learn from that upward movement:

> "I am greatly afflicted";
> I said in my consternation,
> "Men are all a vain hope."
> What shall I render to the Lord
> for all his bounty to me?
> I will lift up the cup of salvation
> and call on the name of the Lord.
> I will pay my vows to the Lord
> in the presence of all his people
> . . . Praise the Lord!
>
> (Ps 116.10–14; 19)

> For I eat ashes like bread,
> and mingle tears with my drink,
> because of thy indignation and anger;
> for thou hast taken me up and thrown me
> away.
> My days are like an evening shadow;
> I wither away like grass.
> But thou, O Lord, art enthroned forever;
> thy name endures to all generations.
> Thou wilt arise and have pity on Zion;

167

. . . For the Lord will build up Zion,
he will appear in his glory;
he will regard the prayer of the destitute,
and will not despise their supplication.

(Ps 102.9–13; 16)

This is the shape of human experience in God. We are made "little less than God" and "crowned with glory and honor." Yet we sin: "I know my transgressions, and my sin is ever before me" (Ps 51.3). Furthermore immorality is all around us: "Rescue me, O my God, from the hand of the wicked, from the grasp of the unjust and cruel man" (Ps 71.4). And *therefore:* "Thou, O Lord, art my hope, my trust, O Lord, from my youth. Upon thee I have leaned from my birth; thou art he who took me from my mother's womb. My praise is continually of thee" (Ps 71.5–6).

So we return to our questions: Are we good? Are we bad? Are we defeated? Are we saved? Are we condemned? Does heaven await? As we watch all of this play out in a glorious but damaged world, our experience is mixed, bittersweet, full of both sorrow and joy. The Psalms encapsulate and guide all of this in poetry and prayer.

2. "To Err *Isn't* Human"

There are a number of popular expressions about human nature that I'd like to take issue with. Alexander Pope's dictum "To err is human" has become all-pervasive, as we excuse failures. Someone vindicating a mistake may say, "I'm only human!" Such expressions are understandable. Our daily experience of society reveals a humanity that is weak, limited, irritating, and prone to greed and dishonesty. So there is a sense in which we are right to curb our expectations. On the other hand, these expressions are unacceptable if used to refer to our essential nature.

True humanity is not broken, but whole. Genuine humanity is not sinful but uncompromised. Being fully human means being fully alive, in free, loving, creative communion with God, with one another, and with the created world. *That* is how you define humanity, not through brokenness and rudderless groping. Seen this way, our journey toward being increasingly God-like is commensurate, even synonymous, with our journey towards becoming fully human.

There are expressions about humanity that are closer to the mark. When someone acts cruelly, abusively, or exploitatively, his or her behavior is often (rightly) condemned as "inhuman." After performing a heroically, a rescuer will often (rightly) say of his or her action, "It was the human thing to do." We are recognizing our essential goodness. "Humane" is actually the original version of the word "human." They became separate forms only in the 18th century, when "humane" came to connote—and rightly so!—"compassion" and "benevolence." Now think what it means to "*d*ehumanize": to deprive people of their innate qualities of individuality, liberty, worth, and dignity. Defining our neighbors, our fellows, our colleagues, our workers, our enemies, our antagonists, our refugees and migrants as "other" is a way of dehumanizing them. People dehumanize others to justify depriving them of basic rights, bully them, or kill them. All of these applications of the word human/humane, humanize and dehumanize, are instructive of our innate sense that humanity is, at root, good and worthy of dignity.

So our imperfection does not mean that we are totally depraved. We are still, at our core, upright and virtuous. Although the humanity that we experience around us is constantly compromised—the shabbiness, mediocrity, and sometimes sheer evil can be mind-numbing—it does not define our existence, theologically speaking.

Epilogue

We've been reflecting from the general to the particular—that is, considering "humanity" in order to start thinking about our own selves. That's deliberately how I set out this reflection on human nature. But this can be misleading. If we think only about the whole of humanity as "good" but individual humans as "sinners," we are thinking like Linus in the classic Peanuts comic, who shouted in exasperation, "I love mankind . . . It's people I can't stand!!"

We can't glibly make theologically beautiful statements about the essential goodness of humanity, without recognizing that individuals can be annoying, criminal, or dangerous.

Classical Christian theology accounts for this problem. It insists on defining humanity by its true, genuine nature, and on seeing the deep-set aberrations within human behavior as *distortions* of that nature. All of us distort our true nature, even as we try to live up to its goodness. We are all on our way to *becoming* human. No matter how much someone sins while they are "becoming human," from the divine perspective, they are still "human," which means, good. So Linus's distinction between a beautiful general "mankind" and bad particular "people" doesn't finally work.

The early-third-century Christian theologian Tertullian writes about life in the womb, "That is a human which is going to be one; you have the fruit already in its seed."[2] Even if fetal life does not yet meet all of the characteristics of a fully conscious human, it only needs time. The *potential* to be human *is* being human. To extrapolate further, no matter a person's age, physical or mental state, or stage of emotional and spiritual development, this human being is valued. Fetus, child, or teenager; callous or sensitive; gay or straight; male or female; communicative or mute; kind or murderous: each is a person on the way to being human, a human-in-progress.

Who am I? Together with you, I am a human being, created in God's image, imperfect and constantly deviating from that image, striving to stay the path that was established and shown me by Jesus Christ. So I am also redeemed, forgiven, or rather (since we are temporal beings) constantly *being* redeemed and forgiven, in the love that God manifests in Christ Jesus.

Notes

[1]For a look into the first four centuries of Christian interpretations of the Genesis creation accounts, see Peter C. Bouteneff, *Beginnings: Ancient Christian Readings of the Biblical Creation Narratives* (Grand Rapids, MI: Baker Academic, 2008).

[2]Tertullian, *Apology* 9.6.

2
What Is Sin?

Right is right even if no one is doing it; wrong is wrong even if everyone is doing it.

Augustine of Hippo

"Sin," in its Greek translation (*hamartia*) means "missing the mark," that is, off target. This matters, because Greek was the language of many of the earliest Church fathers, whose thinking shaped much of our most basic theology. If we are at root good yet broken, it makes sense that this Greek-inflected idea of sin actually presumes our goodness: it presupposes that there is a "mark" to be missed. Hitting the target—not missing it—is truly to be human. Remember, sin does not define humanity; goodness does. Whatever sin is, it does not reside at the root of our nature. Our transgressions result from poor aim, misjudgment, skewed priorities. Sin is failure to be true to what we really are. Which is to say:

- Living beings

- Loving God in freedom

- Flourishing in all good things

Sin is a turning away from that. It negates flourishing, loving, being.

Let's contrast that understanding of sin with three of the more common definitions.

1) *"All things are lawful . . ." (1 Cor 10.23a)*

There are those who reject a notion of sin, or rules, altogether. In this view, we should travel through life, taking its enjoyments and bumps in stride. We should avoid feelings of guilt and shame as detrimental to a life well lived.

2) *". . . but not all things are helpful." (1 Cor 10.23b)*

To others, ethics should simply be left to common sense. Your heart knows the right or "helpful" thing to do, so do it. In essence, everything is permitted, other than what your instincts tell you is obviously wrong.

3) *"Thou shalt not . . ."*

Others consider sins as a list of taboos. Do not lie, do not kill, do not fornicate. Although couched in negatives, such lists can be useful. They can act like the rumble strip on a highway, the indentations in the road that cause your car to make a loud "humm" when you veer off course. The Ten Commandments function something like this, since it is mostly a list of "Thou shalt not"s. They played a crucial role in the cultivation of God's people Israel and they continue to act as guidelines for a right life. They point to the fact of "God's law," which can be upheld or transgressed. Israel knew well that in his love for them God provided these laws so his people—and ultimately all people—might live an abundant, true, healthy life.

But a helpful as "thou-shalt-not" lists can be, they are limited. They can make us feel not as though we are traveling along a highway protected by a rumble strip, but through a minefield, paying more attention to avoiding danger than to progressing forward. Such lists also encourage legalism and self-justification. I can say to myself, "Well, I didn't *technically* commit adultery, because we did not consummate the sexual act (though we did everything short of that . . .)."

In contrast, one of the main characteristics of Christ's commandments is to make the law into a much more holistic way of life. Let's explore what Jesus does with commandments, rules, and the concept of sin.

Identifying the Mark

Let's return to the definition of sin as "missing the mark." If that is correct, we ought to devote some serious attention to what "the mark" should be. Let us orient ourselves. We might be missing it because we're not actually aiming right.

There are many ways to identify the target. Our conscience can act as a pointer, but it is not infallible, and sometimes it is fickle. We need a more reliable guide. To the Christian that is Jesus Christ, as we meet him in the Gospels.

Christ *is* the target. He sets the standard, by his life and his death. He also sets some clear, explicit "commandments," in Matthew 5–7. He not only expands on the Ten Commandments, but he also transforms their proscriptive ("thou-shalt-not") spirit into a holistic handbook for living.

Transforming the Commandments in Love

Jesus begins teaching the commandments through affirmation, rather than negation. *Blessed* are those, he says, who live life in life-affirming ways (peacemaking), or experience these kinds of adversities (unjust persecution), yet maintain these attitudes and dispositions (meekness, purity of heart, the thirst for what is right) (Mt 5.1–12).

The affirmations continue as Christ encourages his listeners to continue seasoning the world with the "salt" of their lives, enlightening the world the way a lamp does on a hill (Mt 5.13–16).

Christ then demonstrates that his teachings not only continue the Law of the Old Testament, but elaborate on it. He teaches that "Do not kill" is insufficient. He wants us to become aware of inner dispositions (notably, anger) that could lead to murder. The inner passions miss the mark as thoroughly as the acts do. Same with adultery: allowing lust to take hold of our emotions is wrong, even if it is never consummated in adultery.

Christ's teachings do more than merely upgrading the Decalogue. By focusing on the spirit as much as on the letter of the law, his commandments become part of a whole way of life, informed foremost by love. Which is perhaps why Christ introduces a radical requirement almost entirely absent from the Old Testament: love of the enemy. That is the greatest test of love and, therefore, love's proof.

Teaching the Commandments with Love

The transition from living the "letter of the law" to living the "spirit of the law" is deeply challenging for Christ's hearers. So he teaches them as does a true pastor. When different inquirers approach him about the law, he listens carefully to them. Then he tailors his response based on what they may be ready to hear to guide them on their next step towards Real Life. With love, he moves each person, in a different way, from "letter" to "spirit."

In one such encounter, a man asks Jesus what he is supposed to do to achieve eternal life. Jesus asks whether he has followed the letter of the law in the Ten Commandments. When Christ hears that he had, he "looked upon him, and loved him." He then challenges him to move beyond the letter of the law to fulfill their spirit—by selling his positions to give to the poor (Mk 10.17–22).

To another inquirer, Jesus asks, "What is written in the law? How do you read it?" By acknowledging the existence of multiple readings, he allows the man to tell him what he has learned, so that he can tailor his answer to the man's understanding. The man has learned the heart and spirit of the Decalogue: "You shall love the Lord your God with all your heart, and with all your soul, and with all your strength, and with all your mind; and your neighbor as yourself." So Jesus tells him, "You have answered right; do this, and you will live" (Lk 10.26–28). The man needs no further instruction.

Part of what we learn from these two encounters is that the Old Testament commandments are limited. As signposts, they are a good place to start, but they need to reflect a whole way of life. Their goal is to bring us into a genuine relationship of love with God, and with fellow human beings so that the rest of our lives falls into place. Conversely, you can spend your life avoiding murder, lying, and adultery and still be selfish and uncharitable: a bitter, heartless legalist. If we are righteous without love, as St Paul reminds us, we gain nothing (1 Cor 13.1–3). But if love is truly the measure of your life, then committing murder, lying, covetousness, adultery become unthinkable. You don't even have to forbid them by name.

The Mark

What we learn from the Gospels' descriptions of Christ—and then from St Paul, and the Church Fathers and

Mothers—is not only that "Thou shalt not" becomes "You ought to." The commandments become something that people have to discern for themselves and live into, on the basis of something bigger. The root principle is, "Love God and love one another, including your enemies." With those, the rest will fall into place. You could say that there is barely even a need to explicitly prohibit specific misdeeds such as murder (or even anger), fornication (or lust), lying (or stretching the truth), because none of them satisfies the criterion of love.

Let's return to our task of identifying the "mark" that we "miss" when we sin. We now know we should be thinking not about wrongdoing and darkness but about doing good and focusing on the light. It is good when we act lovingly toward one another, and give of ourselves to each other. It is good to feed the hungry; clothe people wearing rags; visit hospital patients, elderly neighbors, and prisoners. It is good to love and pray for those who love you and even for those who harm you. These are natural repercussions of love. Reflect on such things. As St Paul writes:

> Finally, brothers and sisters, whatever is true, whatever is honorable, whatever is just, whatever is pure,

whatever is lovely, whatever is gracious, if there is any excellence, if there is anything worthy of praise, think about these things. (Phil 4.8)

All of these aspects of the light—purity, justice, honor, grace, praiseworthiness—come down to one icon, the face of Jesus Christ. The perfect representation of the target we are missing when we sin is Christ on the cross, the blameless one who voluntarily gives himself up to death out of love for humanity. He is the icon of divine life, as well as the icon of genuine human life. He is "the mark."

* * *

It can be liberating to understand sin and righteousness in this way. God shows us an icon to try to emulate. Our task is to try to avoid the behaviors and dispositions that make us less-resemble that icon. This places considerable responsibility on each Christian. But until we are ready for this ethic of liberation, we still require pastorally applied rules, canons, and other guideposts. The three classical "types" of ethical thinking—the proscriptive ("Thou shalt not"), the prescriptive ("You ought to"), and the teleological ("here-is-the-mark-to-aim-for")—all are brought together under the rubric of Christ's love. His love is liberating, but the bar is very high: it is Christ on the cross. His is standard we fail to meet. Therefore the Bible reminds us that no one is sinless, no, not one (Eccl 7.20; Rom 3.10; 1 Jn 1.8), except for Christ himself (Heb 4.15).

Sin as a Condition

As we have seen, sin is both an inner disposition (like anger or lust), and an action (like violence or adultery). But throughout the Bible and the life of the Church, sin is also presented as both a condition, as well as a kind of force.

The condition of sin can be compared to sickness. Sickness itself resembles "missing the mark." We know what health looks like, and sickness is a distortion of it. Understanding our transgression in terms of sickness underscores the importance of identifying it, diagnosing it, and taking steps to heal it. Christ is often described as the great physician, with the Church as his hospital. In the Gospels, Christ often acts literally as a physician, healing the paralyzed, the blind, the lame, and the insane. His ministrations have two features. One, he engages in dialogue with these invalids. He asks what they want. Two, he heals their ailment, and with this he also forgives their sins. Spiritual and physical sickness are bound up with each other, and so are spiritual and physical healing.

Keep in mind that the patient did not necessarily fall ill because he or she sinned (see Jn 9.2–3). Even though physical ailments can stem from vices (alcohol can cause cirrhosis) or from unresolved guilt (stress can exacerbate heart disease), the relationship between the two falls into a larger context. Sin, sickness, and death are all connected. Human sin, as a totality, leads to human sickness and eventually death. Mortality creates a fixed limit to of our lives, so that our gains in wealth and power are a zero-sum game, which means that mortality itself also causes us to sin. It is a vicious cycle, and the way to break it begins with identifying the problem.

The condition of sin can also be compared to enslavement (Jn 8.34). In this view, we are effectively bound to patterns of behavior and cycles of obsessive thinking. We are in thrall to our desires for power and gratification. We find ourselves mired in situations where no solution avoids hurting someone. We are subjugated by our rationalizing processes. Moving away from sin moves us toward freedom, which is why the ideas of "freedom" and "liberation" appear so often throughout this book.

Sin as a Force

Sin is also a kind of force or power. Think about the story of Adam and Eve in Paradise, as told in Genesis 2–3. At the time of their "fall," Adam and Eve aren't perfected, fully realized human beings. If they had been, they wouldn't have listened to a talking snake promising them reward for disobedience. But beyond that, we have to ask ourselves what that serpent was doing there. True, a hint of darkness had entered the story earlier when God instructs them about "the tree of the knowledge of good and evil." (What's this "evil" in Paradise?) In Genesis 3.1, the serpent is described as more "subtle" (sometimes translated instead as "wise," "clever," or "crafty") than the other beasts. His entire purpose appears focused on persuading Eve and Adam to oppose God and then to make things worse by justifying themselves before him.

From the start, we humans have had to reckon with malign influences. Being naked and unashamed in a state of innocence did not safeguard us from danger. If anything, such a state makes you more susceptible. Any parent who has watched his or her innocent children begin to negotiate the world, encounter strangers, or explore the Internet, is aware of this fact. So the book of Genesis, which had detailed the "very good" state of the world and its human inhabitants, then begins to narrate a series of declines. From the fall, it moves on to the exile from Paradise, the murder of Abel, the culture of depravity that inspires the flood (and the consequent "reboot" of human and animal life), the Tower of Babel (even after that reboot, people go wrong). The decline takes a turn only with the call of Abraham, which indicates God's promise to redeem us. The rest of the Old Testament is a series of narratives about God's faithful love of his chosen people—who constantly fall away and have to be called back.

Genesis shows, then, that from the beginning there has been a pull towards wrongdoing. Later scriptures and other writings identify that "pull" with the Devil and his demons. But once humanity is under way, it itself becomes a (or *the*) major vehicle in propagating of that evil. The spiritual forces of immorality, the fear of death, and the sins of others make it virtually impossible for anyone not to go astray. "Sins" are individual actions, but "sin" is a force, a sway, an influence, a power. We ignore it at our peril.

We experience that force as temptations to lie, to do violence, or to lust. In disturbing or terrifying mental images or memories. As addictions to chemical substances, to sex, to money, to power, to abusing others. In the legacy of our family lineages and—sometimes in our national identities (slavery and genocide in the Americas, apartheid in South Africa, the Nazi Holocaust in Germany). Sin forms a virtually irresistible force in our lives, simultaneously primordial (stemming from our very beginnings), generational (across familial and national lineage), and personal (acted on by me myself).[1]

All this sets us a theological problem. The "force" of sin is so great that we can hardly be said to be making free choices. We won't retreat from the idea that humanity is essentially good. But are we really perfected free agents who make thoughtful decisions with the benefit of a clear moral compass? That's not what the facts on the ground indicate. We are born in the state of beautiful innocence and are immediately subject to mixed influences. (Even in the womb we might receive toxic substances that sully our image-bearing beauty.) To some extent, it doesn't matter whether we are born into an idyllic commune, an urban street devastated by drug sales and gunfire, a family that is Christian, Muslim, or atheist. Or rather, of course it matters, but in any case the existentially compromised state of society will act somehow on both our outer and inner lives. Our God-given freedom of choice is deeply affected by our socioeconomic status and the complex of influences and necessities around us.

The environment in which we live comprises our external influences. There are also internal influences, often called "passions." Wise persons across the generations, and across religious and philosophical traditions have identified two basic passions: zeal and desire. These are essentially neutral. They can be beneficial, in the form of the zeal for truth, justice, goodness, and the love of God and the other. They are also potentially bad, in the form of uncontrolled anger and objectifying lust, and all that stems from that. We do well to mediate on their effect on our lives. For who among us is immune to the draw of sexual gratification, the lure of money, and the compulsion to personal power and pride? This complex of attractions, inextricably linked with the knowledge and fear of our mortality, constitutes a more or less governing influence on us. Our surrender to that influence is a sign of the brokenness and tragedy of our world. As a result, among us beautiful and good human beings, all created by God in his own image, there is, as we and the Bible have been saying, no one who lives and does not sin.

But—crucially—that doesn't mean that we *are* sin. Nor that "to live means to sin." Nor that there is no step that we can take without transgressing. Nor that the true reality of human nature is wicked. What it does mean is that the humanity we experience in this world is inevitably distorted. Humanity, collectively, falls short of itself. It misses the mark. But that is not the end of the story. The beginning of healing, from our side, rests with our recognizing the fall of humanity and our own personal role in that fall. It is our recognition of ourselves as sinners, in need of healing. This opens the door to the saving love of God.

Notes

[1]*Sin: Primordial, Generational, and Personal* is the title of a memorable series of talks by Fr Thomas Hopko, available on CD (Yonkers: SVS Press, 2008).

Selected Prayers

The Church's prayer tradition stems from Old-Testament psalms and canticles, as well as material composed throughout the Christian period to the present day. It perpetually balances giving God glory and thanks, begging God's protection and help, and confessing ourselves as sinners needing God's mercy. The prayers included here are a small selection chosen for their relevance to the themes in this book.

Canon of Repentance to Our Lord Jesus Christ

A "canon" is a hymn divided into nine odes, or canticles. Each canticle has an inner structure that encompasses introductory hymns, verses, and refrains. Canons may be recited in community or as personal prayer. The precise origin of this Canon of Repentance is unknown, but it pulls no punches about the depth and severity of our sins. In praying it, we throw ourselves on God's mercy. We also ask for the guidance of Mary the *Theotokos* ("birthgiver of God" in Greek). The Canon of repentance focuses on bringing us to awareness of our sins, compunction for them, and repentance. "Repentance" (*metanoia*—Greek for "change of mind") means the shift in our inner orientation, a God-ward refocus of our lives.

This entire hymn is often used privately as we prepare for Holy Communion, the partaking of the Lord's Supper. Whether in liturgical or private use, this Canon is typically prayed as presented here, with introductory prayers, Psalm 51, and the Nicene Creed.

If you are so inclined, I highly recommend seeking out the Canon as it was set to music, sublimely, by Arvo Pärt in his 1997 composition *Kanon Pokajanen*.

* * *

In the name of the Father and of the Son and of the Holy Spirit. Amen.

Glory to You, our God, glory to You.

O Heavenly King, Comforter, Spirit of Truth, Who art everywhere present and fillest all things, Treasury of good things and Giver of Life, come and dwell in us, and cleanse us of all impurity, and save our souls, O Good One.

Trisagion

Holy God, Holy Mighty, Holy Immortal, have mercy on us.

Holy God, Holy Mighty, Holy Immortal, have mercy on us.

Holy God, Holy Mighty, Holy Immortal, have mercy on us.

Glory to the Father, and to the Son, and to the Holy Spirit, Now and ever, and unto the ages of ages. Amen.

O Most Holy Trinity, have mercy on us. O Lord, cleanse us from our sins; O Master, pardon our iniquities; O Holy One, visit and heal our infirmities, for Your name's sake.

Lord, have mercy. Lord have mercy. Lord have mercy.

Glory to the Father, and to the Son, and to the Holy Spirit, Now and ever, and unto the ages of ages. Amen.

Our Father, Who art in the heavens, hallowed be thy name. Thy kingdom come. Thy will be done, on earth as it is in heaven. Give us this day our daily bread. And forgive us our debts as we forgive our debtors. And lead us not into temptation, but deliver us from evil.

Lord, have mercy. *(Twelve times)*

O Come, let us worship God, our King. *(Bow)*

O Come, let us worship and fall down before Christ, our King and God. *(Bow)*

O Come, let us worship and fall down before Christ himself, our King and God. *(Bow)*

Psalm 51

Have mercy on me, O God, according to your steadfast love; according to your abundant mercy, blot out my transgressions. Wash me thoroughly from my iniquity, and cleanse me from my sin. For I know my transgressions, and my sin is ever before me. Against you, you alone, have I sinned, and done what is evil in your sight, so that you are justified in your sentence and blameless when you pass judgement. Indeed, I was born guilty, a sinner when my mother conceived me. You desire truth in the inward being; therefore teach me wisdom in my secret heart. Purge me with hyssop, and I shall be clean; wash me, and I shall be whiter than snow. Let me hear joy and gladness; let the bones that you have crushed rejoice. Hide your face from my sins, and blot out all my iniquities. Create in me a clean heart, O God, and put a new and right spirit within me. Do not cast me away from your presence, and do not take your holy spirit from me. Restore to me the joy of your salvation, and sustain in me a willing spirit. Then I will teach transgressors your ways, and sinners will return to you. Deliver me from bloodshed, O God, O God of my salvation, and my tongue will sing aloud of your deliverance. O Lord, open my lips, and my mouth will declare your praise. For you have no delight in sacrifice; if I were to give a burnt-offering, you would not be pleased. The sacrifice acceptable to God is a broken spirit; a broken and contrite heart, O God, you will not despise. Do good to Zion in your good pleasure; rebuild the walls of Jerusalem, then you will delight in right sacrifices, in burnt-offerings and whole burnt-offerings; then bulls will be offered on your altar.

The Symbol of Faith

I believe in one God, the Father Almighty, Maker of heaven and earth, and of all things visible and invisible. And in one Lord Jesus Christ, the Son of God, the Only-begotten, begotten of the Father before all ages; Light of Light; true God of true God; begotten, not made; of one essence with the Father, by Whom all things were made; Who for us and for our salvation, came down from the heavens, and was incarnate of the Holy Spirit and the Virgin Mary, and became human; And was crucified for us under Pontius Pilate, and suffered, and was buried; And arose again on the third day according to the Scriptures; And ascended into the heavens, and sits at the right hand of the Father; And shall come again, with glory, to judge both the living and the dead; Whose kingdom shall have no end. And in the Holy Spirit, the Lord, the Giver of Life; Who proceeds from the Father; Who with the Father and the Son together is worshipped and glorified; Who spoke by the prophets. I believe in One, Holy, Catholic, and Apostolic Church. I confess one baptism for the remission of sins. I look for the resurrection of the dead, and the life of the age to come. Amen.

The Canon of Repentance

Ode I

Heirmos: When Israel walked on foot in the deep as on dry land, on seeing their pursuer Pharaoh drowned, they cried: Let us sing to God a song of victory.

Have mercy on me, O God, have mercy on me.

Now I, a burdened sinner, have approached You, my Lord and God. But I dare not raise my eyes to heaven. I only pray, saying: Give me understanding, O Lord, that I may weep bitterly over my deeds.

Have mercy on me, O God, have mercy on me.

O woe is me, a sinner! Wretched am I above all people. There is no repentance in me. Give me, O Lord, tears, that I may weep bitterly over my deeds.

Glory to the Father, and to the Son, and to the Holy Spirit.

Foolish, wretched one, you are wasting your time in idleness! Think of your life and turn to the Lord God, and weep bitterly over your deeds.

Now and ever and unto the ages of ages. Amen.

Theotokion: Most pure Mother of God, look upon me, a sinner, and deliver me from the snares of the devil, and guide me to the way of repentance, that I may weep bitterly over my deeds.

Ode III

Heirmos: There is none holy as you, O Lord my God, Who hast exalted the horn of your faithful, O Good One, and hast established us on the rock of your confession.

Have mercy on me, O God, have mercy on me.

When the thrones are set at the dread judgement, then the deeds of all shall be laid bare. There will be woe for sinners being sent to torment! And knowing that, my soul, repent of thine evil deeds.

Have mercy on me, O God, have mercy on me.

The righteous will rejoice, but the sinners will weep. Then no one will be able to help us, but our deeds will condemn us. Wherefore, before the end, repent of your evil deeds.

Glory to the Father, and to the Son, and to the Holy Spirit.

Woe is me, a great sinner, who have defiled myself by my deeds and thoughts. Not a teardrop do I have, because of my hard-heartedness. But now, rise from the earth, my soul, and repent of your evil deeds.

Now and ever and unto the ages of ages. Amen.

Theotokion: Behold, your Son calls, O Lady, and directs us to what is good, yet I, a sinner, always flee from the good. But you, O merciful one, have mercy on me, that I may repent of mine evil deeds.

Lord, have mercy. Lord, have mercy. Lord, have mercy.

Sedalen: I think of the terrible day and weep over my evil deeds. How shall I answer the Immortal King? With what boldness shall I, a prodigal, look at the Judge? O Kindly Father, O Only-begotten Son, and Holy Spirit, have mercy on me.

Glory to the Father, and to the Son, and to the Holy Spirit, Now and ever, and unto the ages of ages. Amen.

Theotokion: Bound now with many fetters of sins, and inhibited by cruel passions, I flee unto you, my salvation, and cry aloud: Help me, O Virgin, Mother of God.

Ode IV

Heirmos: Christ is my power, my God and my Lord, the august Church sings in godly fashion, and she cries out with a pure mind, keeping festival in the Lord.

Have mercy on me, O God, have mercy on me.

Broad is the way here and convenient for indulging in pleasures, but how bitter it will be on the last day when the soul is separated from the body! Beware of these things, for the sake of the kingdom of God.

Have mercy on me, O God, have mercy on me.

Why do you wrong the poor? Why do you withhold the wage of the hired servant? Why do you not love your brother? Why do you pursue lust and pride? Therefore, abandon these things, my soul, and repent for the sake of the kingdom of God.

Glory to the Father, and to the Son, and to the Holy Spirit.

O mindless one! How long will you busy yourself like a bee, collecting your wealth? For it will perish like dust and ashes soon. But seek rather the kingdom of God.

Now and ever and unto the ages of ages. Amen.

Theotokion: O Lady Theotokos, have mercy on me, a sinner, and strengthen and keep me in virtue, lest sudden death snatch me away unprepared. Lead me, O Virgin, to the kingdom of God.

Ode V

Heirmos: With Your divine light, O Good One, illumine the souls of them that rise early to pray to You with love, I pray, that they may know You, O Word of God, as the true God, Who recalls us from the darkness of sin.

Have mercy on me, O God, have mercy on me.

Remember, wretched one, how you are enslaved to lies, calumnies, theft, infirmities, wild beasts, on account of sins. O my sinful soul, is this what you have desired?

Have mercy on me, O God, have mercy on me.

My members tremble, for with all of them I have done wrong: with my eyes in looking, with my ears in hearing, with my tongue in speaking evil, and by surrendering the whole of myself to Gehenna. O my sinful soul, is this what you have desired?

Glory to the Father, and to the Son, and to the Holy Spirit.

You received the prodigal and the thief who repented, O Saviour, and I alone have succumbed to sinful sloth and have become enslaved to evil deeds. O my sinful soul, is this what you have desired?

Now and ever and unto the ages of ages. Amen.

Theotokion: Wonderful and speedy helper of all, help me, O Mother of God, unworthy as I am, for my sinful soul hath desired this.

Ode VI

Heirmos: Beholding the sea of life surging with the tempest of temptations, I run to Your calm heaven and cry unto You: Raise up my life from corruption, O Greatly-merciful One.

Have mercy on me, O God, have mercy on me.

I have lived my life wantonly on earth and have delivered my soul to darkness. But now I implore You, O merciful Lord, free me from this work of the enemy and give me the knowledge to do Your will.

Have mercy on me, O God, have mercy on me.

Who does such things as I do? For like a swine lying in the mud, so do I serve sin. But pull me out of this vileness, O Lord, and give me the heart to do your commandments.

Glory to the Father, and to the Son, and to the Holy Spirit.

Rise, wretched one, to God and, remembering your sins, fall down before your Creator, weeping and groaning, for He is merciful and will grant you to know His will.

Now and ever and unto the ages of ages. Amen.

Theotokion: O virgin Mother of God, protect me from evil visible and invisible, O immaculate one, and accept my prayers and convey them to your Son, that He may grant me the mind to do His will.

Have mercy on me, O God, have mercy on me.

Lord, have mercy. Lord, have mercy. Lord, have mercy.

Glory to the Father, and to the Son, and to the Holy Spirit,
Now and ever, and unto the ages of ages. Amen.

Kontakion

O my soul, why do you become rich in sins? Why do you do the will of the devil? On what do you set your hope? Cease from these things and turn to God with weeping, and cry out: O Kind-hearted Lord, have mercy on me, a sinner.

Ikos

Think, my soul, of the bitter hour of death and the judgement day of your God and Creator. For terrible angels will seize you, my soul, and will lead you into the eternal fire. And so, before your death, repent and cry: O Lord, have mercy on me, a sinner.

Ode VII

Heirmos: An Angel made the furnace sprinkle dew on the righteous youths. But the command of God consumed the Chaldeans and prevailed upon the tyrant to cry: Blessed are you, O God of our fathers.
Have mercy on me, O God, have mercy on me.
Put not your hope, my soul, in corruptible wealth, and for what is unjustly collected. For you do not know

to whom you will leave it all. But cry: "O Christ our God, have mercy on me, who am unworthy."

Have mercy on me, O God, have mercy on me.

Trust not, my soul, in health of body and quickly-passing beauty. For you see that the strong and the young die. But cry aloud: "O Christ our God, have mercy on me, who am unworthy."

Glory to the Father, and to the Son, and to the Holy Spirit.

Remember, my soul, eternal life and the heavenly kingdom prepared for the saints, and the outer darkness and the wrath of God for the evil, and cry: O Christ, our God, have mercy on me, who am unworthy.

Now and ever and unto the ages of ages. Amen.

Theotokion: Fall down, my soul, before the Mother of God, and pray to her; for she is the quick helper of those that repent. She entreats the Son, Christ God, and has mercy on me, who am unworthy.

Ode VIII

Heirmos: From the flame you sprinkled dew upon the Saints, and burned the sacrifice of a righteous man which was sprinkled with water. For you alone, O Christ, do all as You will. We exalt You unto all ages.

Have mercy on me, O God, have mercy on me.

How shall I not weep when I think of death? For I have seen my brother in his coffin, without glory or comeliness. What then am I to expect? And what do I hope for? Only grant me, O Lord, repentance before the end.

Glory to the Father, and to the Son, and to the Holy Spirit.

I believe that you will come to judge the living and the dead, and that all will stand in order, old and young, lords and princes, priests and virgins. Where shall I find myself? Therefore, I cry: grant me, O Lord, repentance before the end.

Now and ever, and unto the ages of ages. Amen.

Theotokion: O most pure Theotokos, accept mine unworthy prayer and preserve me from sudden death; and grant me repentance before the end.

Ode IX

Heirmos: It is not possible for men to see God, on Whom the ranks of angels dare not gaze; but through you, O all-pure one, the Word Incarnate appeared to us, whom magnifying, with the heavenly hosts we call you blessed.

Have mercy on me, O God, have mercy on me.

207

I now flee unto you, O Angels, Archangels, and all the heavenly hosts who stand at the throne of God: pray to your Creator that He may save my soul from eternal torment.

Have mercy on me, O God, have mercy on me.

Now I turn to you with tears, holy patriarchs, kings and prophets, apostles and holy hierarchs, and all the elect of Christ: Help me at the judgment, that He may save my soul from the power of the enemy.

Glory to the Father, and to the Son, and to the Holy Spirit.

Now I lift my hands to you, holy martyrs, hermits, virgins, righteous ones and all the saints, who pray to the Lord for the whole world, that He may have mercy on me at the hour of my death.

Now and ever, and unto the ages of ages. Amen.

Theotokion: O Mother of God, help me who have strong hope in you; implore your Son that He may place me on His right hand, unworthy as I am, when He sits to judge the living and the dead. Amen.

Prayer after the Canon

O Master Christ God, Who has healed my passions through Your Passion, and has cured my wounds through Your wounds, grant me, who have sinned greatly against You, tears of compunction. Transform my body with the fragrance of Your live-giving Body, and sweeten my soul with Your precious Blood from the bitterness with which the foe has fed me. Lift up my downcast mind to You, and take it out of the abyss of perdition, for I have no repentance, have no compunction, I have no consoling tears, which uplift children to their heritage. My mind has been darkened through earthly passions, I cannot look up to You in pain. I cannot warm myself with tears of love for You. But, O Sovereign Lord Jesus Christ, Treasury of good things, give me thorough repentance and a diligent heart to seek You; grant me Your grace, and renew in me the likeness of your image. I have forsaken you—do not forsake me! Come out to seek me; lead me up to your pasturage and number me among the sheep of your chosen flock. Nourish me with them on the grass of your Holy Mysteries, through the intercessions of your most pure Mother and all your saints. Amen.

Evlogitaria: Requiem Hymns

These hymns are sung at funeral and memorial services. They focus less on the dead person than on ourselves. They help us pray to be taught the ways of God, so that we may be called back from our sin to our true, image-bearing glory.

* * *

Blessed are You, O Lord, teach me Your
    statutes.
The choir of the saints have found the fountain
    of life and
the door of paradise.
May I also find the way through repentance.
I am a lost sheep: call me, O Savior, and save
    me.

Blessed are You, O Lord, teach me Your
    statutes.
For preaching the Lamb of God,
You holy martyrs were led as lambs to
    slaughter.

You have been received into unfading and
    everlasting life.
Now entreat the Lord to grant us forgiveness
    of sins.

*Blessed are You, O Lord, teach me Your
    statutes.*
"You that have walked the narrow way of
    grief:
You that have borne the cross as your yoke in
    life,
You that have followed Me by faith;
Draw near and receive the heavenly crowns I
    have prepared
for you."

*Blessed are You, O Lord, teach me Your
    statutes.*
I am the image of Your ineffable glory,
Though I bear the brands of transgressions:
Pity Your creature, O Master,
And purify me by Your loving-kindness;
Grant me the homeland of my heart's desire,
Making me again a citizen of Paradise.

*Blessed are You, O Lord, teach me Your
statutes.*
O You Who of old formed me from
nothingness,
And honored me with Your image divine,
But by the transgression of Your
commandment
You have returned me again unto the earth
from which I was taken:
Restore me to that image, and to my former
beauty.

*Blessed are You, O Lord, teach me Your
statutes.*
Give rest, to the souls of Your servants, O God,
And establish them in Paradise.
Where the choirs of the saints, and of the just,
O Lord,
Shine like the stars of heaven.
Give rest to Your servants who have fallen
asleep,
Overlooking all their transgressions.

*Glory to the Father, and to the Son, and to the
Holy Spirit.*

Let us praise the three-fold Splendor of the one
    Godhead, crying:
Holy are You, O Father, Who without
    beginning,
Coeternal Son and divine Spirit!
Enlighten us who serve You in faith;
And deliver us from eternal fire.

Now, and ever, and unto ages of ages. Amen.

Rejoice O exalted Lady.
You gave birth to God in the flesh for the
    salvation of all.
Through you may we find Paradise,
O pure, most blessed Theotokos.
Alleluia, Alleluia, Alleluia, glory to You, O God.
Alleluia, Alleluia, Alleluia, glory to You, O God.
Alleluia, Alleluia, Alleluia, glory to You, O God.

The Jesus Prayer

Now that we have reproduced hymns and prayers of various lengths, here is a very short one—and probably one of the best known of all Orthodox prayers. (Among other works, it plays vital roles not only in *The Way of the Pilgrim* but also J.D. Salinger's *Franny and Zooey*.) Its simplicity and brevity makes it supremely adaptable. You can repeat it however often you like during time you've set aside for prayer and quiet. You can also say it at random times throughout the day. It can be especially useful while waiting—for a train, a doctor, a friend, or sleep—but can accompany anything you are doing. It is an excellent substitute for inner chatter or spiraling thoughts. Truly, it is the best place to park your mind. It adapts to gratitude, fear, joy, sadness, regret, compunction, and directionlessness. By orienting us to Jesus Christ, it stills and focuses the mind and the body, bringing both into a godly peace.

Short as the Jesus prayer is, it sums up the basics about our life and our salvation. It is both a confession of faith and a confession of sin. It identifies Jesus Christ as the Son of God and the one praying as a sinner. What links these two antitheses—God and sinner—is mercy.

* * *

Lord Jesus Christ, Son of God,
have mercy on me, a sinner.